MW00617435

Motorbooks International

TRI-CHEVY
RED BOOK

Peter C. Sessler

First published in 1992 by Motorbooks International
Publishers & Wholesalers, PO Box 2, 729 Prospect Avenue,
Osceola, WI 54020 USA

Motorbooks International is a certified trademark, registered
with the United States Patent Office

The information in this book is true and complete to the best
of our knowledge. All recommendations are made without
any guarantee on the part of the author or Publisher, who
also disclaim any liability incurred in connection with the use
of this data or specific details

All photos courtesy of Chevrolet Motor Division

We recognize that some words, model names and
designations, for example, mentioned herein are the property
of the trademark holder. We use them for identification
purposes only. This is not an official publication

Motorbooks International books are also available at
discounts in bulk quantity for industrial or sales-promotional
use. For details write to Special Sales Manager at the
Publisher's address

Library of Congress Cataloging-in-Publication Data
Sessler, Peter C.
    Tri-Chevy red book / Peter C. Sessler.
      p.   cm.—(Motorbooks International red book series)
    ISBN 0-87938-625-8
    1. Chevrolet automobile—Collectors and collecting.
  2. Chevrolet automobile—Parts.   3. Chevrolet
automobile—Specifications.
  I. Title.   II. Series.
TL215.C5S48   1992
629.222—dc20   92-23626

On the front cover: A 1957 Bel Air convertible owned by
Bruce and Linda Finley. *Mike Mueller*

On the back cover: A 1955 Bel Air Sport Coupe. *Chevrolet*

Printed and bound in the United States of America

Contents

Special thanks to Bob Hall, Paul McLaughlin, Mark Roderick, Fred Sherman, Classic Chevy Club International, and Chevrolet Motor Division.

Introduction

This book is designed to help the Chevy enthusiast determine the authenticity and originality of any Chevrolet 150, 210, and Bel Air produced between 1955 and 1957. Each chapter covers a model year and includes production figures; vehicle identification number (VIN) decoding information; basic engine specifications, engine and transmission suffix codes; carburetor, distributor, coil, generator, regulator, and starter motor numbers; option order codes and retail prices; dealer-installed accessories and retail prices; exterior color and interior trim codes and combinations; convertible top color codes; and selected facts. An appendix lists additional information such as how to identify engines, transmissions, and rear axles, how to decode engine cowl tags, and how to decipher engine casting date codes.

The 1955–57 Chevrolets have become the most popular of any postwar Chevrolet collectibles. The 1955–57 models represented a departure from past Chevrolet cars in terms of styling and performance. Clearly, these cars were more exciting, and almost 5 million were sold in three years. Unquestionably, they have become modern classics, with the 1957s attaining cult status. Today, these cars have a large, organized following as well as a responsive industry offering a host of reproduction parts that make their restoration fairly easy.

A considerable number of these cars have been modified, but it is the stock or close-to-stock cars that offer more as an investment, especially the Bel Air models. As with other high-dollar collectibles, be sure of what you're looking at.

For the enthusiast, the most important number in any Chevrolet is its VIN, which was stamped on a metal plate and attached to the driver's-side door pillar. On 1955–57 Chevrolets, it consisted of ten digits for six-cylinder-equipped cars and eleven digits for V-8s, which broke down to model series, model year, assembly plant, and consecutive unit number. You could not tell which engine came in a particular car, only whether the car was equipped with a six- or eight-cylinder unit.

Although you can't match the engine to the chassis it was installed in, you can at least determine if the engine installed is correct or not. The 1955–56 engines were stamped with an engine serial number that included the plant, the model year, the unit number, and a suffix code, which indicated engine size and application. In 1957, the model year code was dropped and replaced with four digits that indicated the date and month the engine was built. For both 1955–56 and 1957 cars, the engine blocks, heads, and so forth were also cast with date codes that showed when they were cast. When these are combined with the production dates listed in the Appendix, you should be able to determine to a large degree whether or not the engine installed in a particular car is correct.

Even if all the numbers match on a particular car you are looking at, it will be to your advantage if the car is documented. It is all the better if the previous owner can provide you with the original invoice or window sticker, any service records, and the like. This is especially important with the rare, popular models, such as 1957 Bel Air convertibles.

The colors and interior trims listed in each chapter are correct as far as they go. However, Chevrolet did build cars in colors and trim combinations not listed. As with all the information listed here, be open to the possibility that exceptions can and do occur. This means that you'll have to work harder to determine authenticity.

Every effort has been made to make sure that the information contained in this book is correct. However, I would like to hear from enthusiasts with any corrections or interesting additions. Please write to me care of Motorbooks International.

Chapter 1

1955 Chevrolet

Production

Model	Number Built	Percentage of Total
150 Series, 6cyl & 8cyl		
1502 2dr sedan	66,833	3.76
1503 4dr sedan	34,906	1.96
1508 2dr sedan delivery	10,639	0.60
1512 2dr utility sedan	12,139	0.68
1529 2dr Handyman station wagon	18,496	1.04
Total	143,013	8.04
210 Series, 6cyl & 8cyl		
2102 2dr sedan	250,000	14.07
2103 4dr sedan	340,222	19.15
2109 4dr Townsman station wagon	84,239	4.74
2124 2dr Delray club coupe	116,406	6.55
2129 2dr Handyman station wagon	29,419	1.66
2154 2dr hardtop sport coupe	11,685	0.66
Total	831,971	46.83
Bel Air Series, 6cyl & 8cyl		
2402 2dr sedan	168,826	9.50
2403 4dr sedan	366,293	20.63
2409 4dr Beauville station wagon	25,772	1.45
2429 2dr Nomad station wagon	8,530	0.48
2434 2dr convertible	42,278	2.38
2454 2dr hardtop sport coupe	189,269	10.65
Total	800,968	45.09

Model	Number Built	Percentage of Total
Corvette		
2934 2dr convertible	700	0.04
Grand Total	1,776,652	100.00

Serial Numbers

Description
VC55F001001

V—V-8 engine (no letter V–6cyl engine)

C—Car series (A–150 Series, B–210 Series, C–Bel Air Series, D–sedan delivery series)

55—Last two digits of model year

F—Assembly plant (A–Atlanta, B–Baltimore, F–Flint, J–Janesville, K–Kansas City, L–Los Angeles, N–Norwood, O–Oakland, S–St. Louis, T–Tarrytown)

001001—Consecutive sequence number

Location
On stainless steel plate that is spot welded on left front door hinge post.

Basic Engine Specifications
(Horsepower/torque output)

235ci Blue Flame 123 6cyl—123 gross hp @ 3800rpm/207lb-ft @ 2000rpm; 109 net hp @ 3600rpm/195lb-ft @ 2000rpm

235ci Blue Flame 136 6cyl—136 gross hp @ 4200rpm/209lb-ft @ 2200rpm; 121 net hp @ 3800rpm/195lb-ft @ 2000rpm

265ci Turbo-Fire 2bbl V-8—162 gross hp @ 4400rpm/257lb-ft @ 2200rpm; 137 net hp @ 4000rpm/235lb-ft @ 2200rpm

265ci Turbo-Fire 4bbl V-8—180 gross hp @ 4600rpm/260lb-ft @ 2800rpm; 160 net hp @ 4200rpm/240lb-ft @ 2600rpm

Engine and Transmission Suffix Codes
Z—235ci 6cyl 123hp, 3-speed manual & overdrive

ZC—235ci 6cyl 123hp, HD clutch

ZH—235ci 6cyl 123hp, 3-speed, aluminum camshaft gear

ZJ—235ci 6cyl 123hp, HD clutch, aluminum camshaft gear
Y—235ci 6cyl 136hp, Powerglide automatic
G—265ci V-8 162hp, 3-speed manual
GC—265ci V-8 162hp, overdrive
GF—265ci V-8 162hp, 3-speed w/AC
GQ—265ci V-8 162hp, overdrive w/AC
GK—265ci V-8 162hp, HD clutch w/AC
F—265ci V-8 162hp, Powerglide
FC—265ci V-8 162hp, Powerglide automatic w/AC
GL—265ci V-8 180hp, 3-speed, dual exhaust, 4bbl carburetor
GM—265ci V-8 180hp, 3-speed, dual exhaust, 4bbl carburetor, AC
GE—265ci V-8 180hp, overdrive, dual exhaust, 4bbl carburetor
GN—265ci V-8 180hp, overdrive, dual exhaust, 4bbl carburetor, AC
FB—265ci V-8 180hp, Powerglide, dual exhaust, 4bbl carburetor
FD—265ci V-8 180hp, Powerglide, dual exhaust, 4bbl carburetor, AC

Carburetors
235ci 6cyl—7007181
265ci V-8 162hp, 7008005 (Manual transmission)
265ci V-8 162hp, 7008004 (Powerglide transmission)
265ci V-8 180hp—Carter WCFB 2351S

Distributors
235ci 6cyl—1102403
265ci 8cyl—1110847

Coils
235ci 6cyl—1115085
265ci 8cyl—1115083

Generators
25amp for 235/265ci—1100310
30amp for 235/265ci—1102014
40amp (low–cut-in) for 235/265ci—1106981

Regulators

25amp for 235/265ci—1118945
30amp for 235/265ci—1118826
40amp (low–cut-in) for 235/265ci—1118948

Starting Motors

235ci 6cyl—1107626
265ci 8cyl—1107627

Option Order Codes (Including Factory D&H) and Retail Prices

Model	6cyl	8cyl
150 Series		
1502 2dr sedan	$1,660.00	$1,759.00
1503 4dr sedan	1,703.00	1,802.00
1512 2dr utility sedan	1,568.00	1,667.00
1529 2dr Handyman station wagon	2,005.00	2,104.00
210 Series		
2102 2dr sedan	1,750.00	1,849.00
2103 4dr sedan	1,794.00	1,893.00
2109 4dr Townsman station wagon	2,102.00	2,201.00
2124 2dr Delray club coupe	1,810.00	1,909.00
2129 2dr Handyman station wagon	2,054.00	2,153.00
Bel Air Series		
2402 2dr sedan	1,863.00	1,962.00
2403 4dr sedan	1,907.00	2,006.00
2409 4dr Beauville station wagon	2,237.00	2,336.00
2434 2dr convertible	2,181.00	2,280.00
2454 2dr hardtop sport coupe	2,042.00	2,141.00

Option Order Codes and Retail Prices

100	Directional signal	$16.75
101B	Airflow heater (NA w/AC)	72.80
101C	Recirculating heater (NA w/AC)	48.15
216C	1-pint-capacity oil bath air cleaner (6cyl only)	5.40
227A	HD clutch	3.25

235	Single colors	NC
235W	Single color—Anniversary Gold 2403 only	26.90
236G, M	Single colors	NC
236A, F, H	Special two-tone combinations	25.85
237B	1-quart-capacity oil filter (6cyl)	11.85
237L	1-quart-capacity oil filter (8cyl)	11.85
237M	1-quart-capacity oil filter (w/AC)	14.00
238A, F, P, W	Special two-tone combinations	25.85
238H, M, N, U	Single colors	NC
238G, K, L, Q, S, T, V, X	Standard two-tone combinations	12.95
241A	Governor (std w/6cyl)	18.30
246	Two-tone color combinations	12.95
254T	HD 5-leaf rear springs	2.70
254Y	HD rear springs (station wagons)	3.80
254V	HD 6-leaf rear springs	6.50
288A	5 6.70-15-6 tires	37.90
288L	5 6.70-15-6 white-sidewall tires	73.65
290B	5 6.70-15-4 white-sidewall tires	26.90
313	Powerglide transmission	178.35
315	Overdrive transmission	107.60
320	Electric windshield wiper	10.50
324	Power steering	91.50
325A, B, L, N, P	30amp generator	7.55
325U–Z	30amp generator	NC
325C–F, Q, R	40amp generator	80.75
397	Seat & window electrical controls	145.30

Option Order Codes and Retail Prices

398	E-Z Eye glass	32.30
410	4bbl carburetor	59.20
412	Power brakes	37.70
417	Positive engine venti-lation	12.95
435	Trim combination	NC
437	Single colors	NC
440	Single colors	NC
441	Two-tone color com-binations	12.95
450	AC	565.00

Dealer-installed Accessories and Retail Prices (Excluding Installation Charges)

Autotronic Eye	$44.25
Cap—locking gas	2.90
Carrier—Continental wheel	118.00
Clock—electric	17.50
Compass	3.57
Covers—full wheel, set of 4	14.95
Covers—wheel disc, set of 4	19.00
Cover—seat, plastic	34.90
Cover—seat, plastic Spring Line	37.50
Cover—seat, fiber	26.90
Cover—seat, nylon	39.90
Cover—seat, nylon Spring Line	42.50
Dispenser—tissues	3.85
Extension—exhaust	3.25
Glareshade—windshield, 1	8.00
Guards—front & rear fender	39.00
Guards—door edge, pair (sport coupe & convertible)	3.45
Guards—door edge, 4dr set	6.25
Guard—gasoline filler door	1.65
Heater & defroster—deluxe	65.00
Heater & defroster—recirculating	42.00
Kool Kooshion	4.40
Lamp—luggage compartment	1.95
Lamp—underhood	1.95
Lamp—courtesy, pair	2.75

Lamp—back-up	5.85
Lamp—glove compartment	1.10
Mat units—floor, rubber, 2	3.50
Mirror—inside rearview, nonglare	3.95
Mirror—outside rearview, body mount	3.50
Mirror—outside rearview, remote control	6.95
Mirror—vanity visor	1.60
Molding—body sill	7.00
Radio & antenna—push-button	84.50
Radio & antenna—manual	62.00
Radio & antenna—Signal Seeker	105.00
Raiser—automatic top	34.00
Rings—wheel trim, 15in, set of 5	11.75
Safetylight & mirror	24.50
Seat & back rest—Sacro-Ease	19.75
Shields—door handle, set of 4	2.80
Shields—gravel, front fender, pair	6.75
Signal—parking brake, electric	4.25
Speaker—rear seat radio	12.00
Spotlight—hand, portable	7.95
Ventshades	8.75
Viewer—traffic light	2.90
Visor—outside	19.90
Washer—windshield, vacuum operated	7.95

One-Color Combinations

Chart split into two sections

Combination Number	Model Usage	Body Color
585	2102, 2103, 2124, 1502, 1503, 1508, 1512, 2402, 2403, 2434, 2454	Onyx Black
586	2102, 2103, 2124, 2402, 2403, 2434, 150 Series	Sea Mist Green
587	2102, 2103, 2124, 2109, 2129, 2402, 2403, 2454, 2419, 150 Series	Neptune Green
588	2102, 2103, 2124, 1502, 1503, 1508, 1512, 2402, 2403, 2434	Skyline Blue

Combination Number	Model Usage	Body Color
589	2102, 2103, 2124, 2109, 2129, 1502, 1503, 1508, 1512, 2402, 2403, 2454, 2419	Glacier Blue
590	2102, 2103, 1502, 1503, 1508, 1512, 2402, 2403	Copper Maroon
591	2102, 2103, 2109, 2129, 1502, 1503, 1512, Bel Air Series	Shoreline Beige
592	2102, 2103, 2109, 2129, 1502, 1503, 1512, 1529, 2434	Autumn Bronze
593	2102, 2103, 2124, 1502, 1503, 1508, 1512, 2402, 2403	India Ivory
594	2102, 2103, 1502, 1503, 1508, 1512, 2402, 2403	Shadow Gray
596	1508, 2434	Gypsy Red
598	2419, 2434	Regal Turquoise
626	2434	Coral
630	2154, 2454	Harvest Gold
683	2102, 2103, 2124, 1502, 1503, 1508, 1512	Cashmere Blue

Combination Number	Model Usage	Wheel Color	Wheel Striping Color
585	2102, 2103, 2124, 1502, 1503, 1508, 1512	Black	Argent Silver
585	2402, 2403, 2434, 2454	Black	None
586	2102, 2103, 2124, 150 Series	Sea Mist Green	Onyx Black
586	2402, 2403, 2434	Sea Mist Green	None

14

587	2102, 2103, 2124, 2109, 2129, 150 Series	Neptune Green	Argent Silver
587	2402, 2403, 2454, 2419	Neptune Green	None
588	2102, 2103, 2124, 1502, 1503, 1508, 1512	Skyline Blue	Onyx Black
588	2402, 2403, 2434	Skyline Blue	None
589	2102, 2103, 2124, 2109, 2129, 1502, 1503, 1508, 1512	Glacier Blue	Argent Silver
589	2402, 2403, 2454, 2419	Glacier Blue	None
590	2102, 2103, 1502, 1503, 1508, 1512	Copper Maroon	Argent Silver
590	2402, 2403	Copper Maroon	None
591	2102, 2103, 2109, 2129, 1502, 1503, 1512	Shoreline Beige	Onyx Black
591	Bel Air Series	Shoreline Beige	None
592	2102, 2103, 2109, 2129, 1502, 1503, 1512, 1529	Autumn Bronze	Argent Silver
592	2434	Autumn Bronze	None
593	2102, 2103, 2124, 1502, 1503, 1508, 1512	India Ivory	Onyx Black
593	2402, 2403	India Ivory	None
594	2102, 2103, 1502, 1503, 1508, 1512	Shadow Gray	Argent Silver
594	2402, 2403	Shadow Gray	None
596	1508, 2434	Gypsy Red	None
598	2419, 2434	Regal Turquoise	None
626	2434	Coral	None
630	2154, 2454	Harvest Gold	None
683	2102, 2103, 2124, 1502, 1503, 1508, 1512	Cashmere Blue	Onyx Black or None

Two-Tone Color Combinations
Chart split into two sections

Combination Number	Model Usage	Upper/Lower Body Colors
599	2102, 2103, 2109, 2129, 1502, 1503, 1529, 2402, 2403	Sea Mist Green/ Neptune Green
600	2102, 2103, 1502, 1503, 2402, 2403	Skyline Blue/ Glacier Blue
601	2154, 2454	Neptune Green/ Shoreline Beige
602	2102, 2103, 2124, 1502, 1503, 2402, 2403, 2454	India Ivory/ Skyline Blue
603	2109, 2129	Autumn Bronze/ Shoreline Beige
604	2409, 2434	Neptune Green/ Sea Mist Green
605	2102, 2103, 2124	India Ivory/ Sea Mist Green
606	2102, 2103, 1529, 2402, 2403, 2419, 2454	Shoreline Beige/ Autumn Bronze
607	2102, 2103, 2124	Glacier Blue/ Shoreline Beige
608	2124, 2402, 2403, 2434, 2454	India Ivory/ Onyx Black
610	2109, 2129, 2134, 2434	Glacier Blue/ Skyline Blue
612	2402, 2403, 2434, 2454	India Ivory/ Regal Turquoise
613	2102, 2103, 1502, 1503, 1512, 2402, 2403, 2454	Shoreline Beige/ Neptune Green
614	2102, 2103, 2124, 2109, 2129, 1502, 1503, 2402, 2403, 2419, 2454	Shoreline Beige/ Glacier Blue
615	2419, 2434, 2454	Shoreline Beige/ Gypsy Red
617	2124	India Ivory/ Gypsy Red

624	2102, 2103, 1502, 1503, 1512, 2402	India Ivory/ Shadow Gray
627	2402, 2403, 2429, 2434, 2454	Shadow Gray/ Coral
628	2124, 2402, 2403, 2454	Onyx Black/ India Ivory
629	2134, 2434	India Ivory/ Coral
631	2124, 2402, 2403, 2434, 2454	India Ivory/ Harvest Gold
682	2102, 2103, 2124, 2109, 2129, 1502, 1503, 2402, 2403, 2419, 2429, 2434, 2454	India Ivory/ Cashmere Blue
684	2102, 2103, 2109, 2129, 1529, 2402, 2403, 2419, 2429, 2434, 2454	India Ivory/ Navaho Tan
685	2402, 2403, 2429, 2434, 2454	India Ivory/ Dusk Rose

Combi-nation Number	Model Usage	Wheel Colors	Wheel Striping Color
599	2102, 2103, 2109, 2129, 1502, 1503, 1529	Neptune Green	Argent Silver
599	2402, 2403	Neptune Green	None
600	2102, 2103, 1502, 1503	Glacier Blue	Argent Silver
600	2402, 2403	Glacier Blue	None
601	2154, 2454	Shoreline Beige	None
602	2102, 2103, 2124, 1502, 1503	Skyline Blue	Onyx Black
602	2402, 2403, 2454	Skyline Blue	None
603	2109, 2129	Shoreline Beige	Onyx Black
604	2409, 2434	Sea Mist Green	None
605	2102, 2103, 2124	Sea Mist Green	Onyx Black
606	2102, 2103, 1529	Autumn Bronze	Argent Silver
606	2402, 2403, 2419, 2454	Autumn Bronze	None

Combination Number	Model Usage	Wheel Colors	Wheel Striping Color
607	2102, 2103, 2124	Shoreline Beige	Onyx Black
608	2124	Black	Argent Silver
608	2402, 2403, 2434, 2454	Black	None
610	2109, 2129	Skyline Blue	Onyx Black
610	2134, 2434	Skyline Blue	None
612	2402, 2403, 2434, 2454	Regal Turquoise	None
613	2102, 2103, 1502, 1503, 1512	Neptune Green	Argent Silver
613	2402, 2403, 2454	Neptune Green	None
614	2102, 2103, 2124, 2109, 2129, 1502, 1503	Glacier Blue	Argent Silver
614	2402, 2403, 2419, 2454	Glacier Blue	None
615	2419, 2434, 2454	Gypsy Red	None
617	2124	Gypsy Red	Argent Silver
624	2102, 2103, 1502, 1503, 1512	Shadow Gray	Argent Silver
624	2402	Shadow Gray	None
627	2402, 2403, 2429, 2434, 2454	Coral	None
628	2124	India Ivory	Onyx Black
628	2402, 2403, 2454	India Ivory	None
629	2134, 2434	Coral	None
631	2124	Harvest Gold	Onyx Black
631	2402, 2403, 2434, 2454	Harvest Gold	None
682	2102, 2103, 2124, 2109, 2129, 1502, 1503	Cashmere Blue	Onyx Black
682	2402, 2403, 2419, 2429, 2434, 2454	Cashmere Blue	None
684	2102, 2103, 2109, 2129, 1529	Navaho Tan	Onyx Black
684	2402, 2403, 2419, 2429, 2434, 2454	Navaho Tan	None
685	2402, 2403, 2429, 2434, 2454	Dusk Rose	None

Interior Trim Combinations

500	Light gray pattern cloth
501	Straw–brown imitation leather
502	Straw–brown imitation leather
503	Light blue pattern cloth–dark blue plain cloth
504	Light green pattern cloth–dark green plain cloth
505	Light tan pattern cloth–dark brown plain cloth
506	Light blue–beige imitation leather
507	Light green–beige imitation leather
508	Black–ivory imitation leather
509	Dark blue pattern cloth–light blue imitation leather
510	Dark green pattern cloth–light green imitation leather
511	Dark brown pattern cloth–beige imitation leather
513	Turquoise pattern cloth–ivory imitation leather
514	Light blue–beige imitation leather
515	Dark green–light green imitation leather
516	Brown–beige imitation leather
517	Beige pattern cloth–beige imitation leather
518	Beige pattern cloth–light blue imitation leather
519	Beige pattern cloth–light blue imitation leather
520	Beige pattern cloth–light green imitation leather
521	Beige pattern cloth–red imitation leather
522	Beige pattern cloth–turquoise imitation leather
524	Dark green–light green imitation leather
525	Red–beige imitation leather
526	Dark green–light green imitation leather
527	Dark blue–light blue imitation leather
528	Brown–beige imitation leather
531	Dark gray pattern cloth–coral imitation leather
532	Gray pattern cloth–coral imitation leather
533	Dark gray–coral imitation leather
537	Turquoise–ivory imitation leather
541	Beige & green leather
542	Beige & blue leather
543	Beige & brown leather
544	Beige & red leather
545	Ivory & turquoise leather
546	Gray & coral leather
547	Light gray–black imitation leather

Interior Trim Combinations

549 Dark gray pattern cloth–ivory imitation leather
550 Gray pattern cloth–ivory imitation leather
551 Dark gray–ivory imitation leather
552 Gray & ivory leather

Exterior Color and Interior Trim Combinations

150 Series

	Interior Trim		
Exterior Color	**1502, 1503, 1512**	**1529**	**1508**
585 Onyx Black	547	—	501
586 Sea Mist Green	547	524	501
587 Neptune Green	547	524	501
588 Skyline Blue	547	—	501
589 Glacier Blue	547	—	501
590 Copper Maroon	547	—	—
591 Shoreline Beige	547	—	—
592 Autumn Bronze	547	502	—
593 India Ivory	547	—	501
594 Shadow Gray	547	—	501
596 Gypsy Red	—	—	501
599 Sea Mist Green/ Neptune Green	547	—	—
600 Skyline Blue/ Glacier Blue	547	—	—
602 India Ivory/ Skyline Blue	547	—	—
613 Shoreline Beige/ Neptune Green	547	—	—
624 India Ivory/ Shadow Gray	547	—	—

210 Series

	Interior Trim		
Exterior Color	**2102, 2103**	**2124**	**2109, 2129**
585 Onyx Black	503	508	—
586 Sea Mist Green	504	507	—

Exterior Color			
587 Neptune Green	504	507	515
588 Skyline Blue	503	506	—
589 Glacier Blue	503	506	514
590 Copper Maroon	505	—	—
591 Shoreline Beige	505	—	—
592 Autumn Bronze	505	—	516
593 India Ivory	503	508	—
594 Shadow Gray	503	—	—
599 Sea Mist Green/ Neptune Green	504	—	—
600 Skyline Blue/ Glacier Blue	503	—	—
602 India Ivory/ Skyline Blue	503	506	—
605 India Ivory/ Sea Mist Green	504	507	—
606 Shoreline Beige/ Autumn Bronze	505	—	—
607 Glacier Blue/ Shoreline Beige	503	506	—
608 India Ivory/ Onyx Black	—	508	—
613 Shoreline Beige/ Neptune Green	504	—	—
617 India Ivory/ Gypsy Red	—	508	—
624 India Ivory/ Shadow Gray	503	—	—
628 Onyx Black/ India Ivory	—	508	—
631 India Ivory/ Harvest Gold	—	507	—

Bel Air Series

	Interior Trim			
Exterior Color	**2402, 2403**	**2409**	**2434**	**2454**
585 Onyx Black	509	—	525	521
586 Sea Mist Green	510	—	—	—
587 Neptune Green	510	—	—	517
588 Skyline Blue	509	—	—	—
589 Glacier Blue	509	518	—	519

Bel Air Series

Exterior Color	Interior Trim			
	2402, 2403	2409	2434	2454
590 Copper Maroon	511	—	—	—
591 Shoreline Beige	511	518	—	521
593 India Ivory	509	—	—	—
594 Shadow Gray	509	—	—	—
596 Gypsy Red	—	517	525	—
598 Regal Turquoise	—	517	—	—
599 Sea Mist Green/ Neptune Green	510	—	—	—
600 Skyline Blue/ Glacier Blue	509	—	—	—
601 Neptune Green/ Shoreline Beige	—	—	—	520
602 India Ivory/ Skyline Blue	509	—	—	519
604 Neptune Green/ Sea Mist Green	—	—	526	—
606 Shoreline Beige/ Autumn Bronze	511	—	528	—
610 Glacier Blue/ Skyline Blue	—	—	527	—
612 India Ivory/ Regal Turquoise	513	—	537	522
613 Shoreline Beige/ Neptune Green	510	—	—	520
614 Shoreline Beige/ Glacier Blue	—	—	—	519
615 Shoreline Beige/ Gypsy Red	—	—	525	521
624 India Ivory/ Shadow Gray	509	—	—	—
626 Coral	—	—	533	—
627 Shadow Gray/Coral	531	—	—	532
629 India Ivory/Coral	—	—	533	—
630 Harvest Gold	—	—	—	520
631 India Ivory/ Harvest Gold	510	—	526	520

Convertible Top Colors
White
Beige
Blue
Green

Facts

The 1955 Chevrolet line was completely restyled and reengineered, although new versions were offered in the three familiar model designations: 150 Series, 210 Series, and Bel Air Series. Unlike other 1955 offerings and the 1954 Chevrolet models, the 1955 Chevrolets were distinguished by a relatively simple rectangular grille, wraparound windshield, hooded headlights, and two-level bodyside accentuation styling on the 210s and Bel Airs.

The 150 Series was available as two- and four-door sedans, a two-door utility sedan that had a raised rear floor without a seat, and a two-door Handyman station wagon. Also part of the 150 Series was a panel sedan delivery, which resembled the two-door wagon without the rear side windows. In keeping with its Spartan image, the 150 Series was almost devoid of any chrome or bright exterior embellishment and came with small hubcaps. In the interior, it came with a rubber floor mat instead of carpeting, a two-spoke steering wheel, and a visor for the driver only. Features such as ashtrays, a cigarette lighter, coat hooks, and armrests weren't standard equipment.

The 210s were available as two- and four-door sedans, a two-door Delray club coupe, a two-door Handyman station wagon, and a four-door Townsman station wagon. A two-door sport coupe was added in June 1955, making a total of six variations. The 210s came with stainless steel trim around the windshield, side windows, and rear windows and with bright moldings running down the side notch from the rear windows and connecting with a rear quarter panel side molding, which set the car off. The wagons did not have the beltline notch but were set off by a horizontal rear molding topped by a winged spear. Hubcaps were also used. In the interior, rubber mats were still used but the cars got chrome front seat and sidewall moldings, a glove compartment light, a cigarette lighter and ashtray, a rear ashtray, automatic dome light switches, foam seats, dual visors, armrests, assist straps, and coat hooks (except on the two-door wagon). The steering wheel was a two-spoke design with a horn ring rather than the horn button used on the 150 Series.

The top of the line was the Bel Air Series. This was available as two- and four-door sedans, a two-door sport coupe, a four-door Beauville station wagon, a convertible, and a two-door Nomad wagon, which was added to the line-up in February 1955. The Bel Airs came with additional bright and chrome exterior trim. The horizontal rear side moldings, which were similar to those on the 210s, were wider and were painted white in the center. Whereas the 150s and 210s had Chevrolet script on each front fender, the Bel Airs got a Chevrolet emblem and Bel Air script above the horizontal rear side molding behind the vertical side spear. The Bel Airs also came with full wheel covers. In the interior, they got floor carpets, a three-spoke steering wheel and horn ring, and an electric clock plus other interior upgrades such as ashtrays, armrests, and so forth.

The most unique 1955 Chevrolet was the Bel Air Nomad two-door wagon. Its styling originated from the Corvette Nomad show car, but it shared many of the regular 1955 production pieces. The Nomad's hood, front fenders, grille, and bumpers were regular production items, but the doors were slightly different from the production hardtop doors, as they did not have the characteristic beltline notch. The windshield and side vent windows were regular production, but the rear side windows and the liftgate glass were unique. The rear quarter panels were also different, as were the tailgate and liftgate. The liftgate was chrome-plated, and the tailgate got seven chrome strips. Early Nomads came with a handle on the center tailgate strip and chrome-plated outside reveal moldings on the rear quarter windows, whereas later Nomads got stainless steel outside reveal moldings. The roof on the Nomad was distinctive—it was ribbed with nine grooves. The Nomad also differed from regular production cars by its chrome headlamp eyebrow and white insert side trim on the front fender, larger rear wheel cutouts, and a special interior that used a waffle and ribbed vinyl trim. The Bel Air script and Chevrolet emblem were relocated on the rear fender behind the taillights. Nomad script was used on the tailgate.

Two-tone paint treatments were optional on all three model series. The 150s and 210s with the two-tone paint got their roof painted a different color, and the Bel Airs got the roof, rear deck, and upper rear quarter panel areas painted a contrasting color.

The 1955 Chevrolet benefited through the use of a lighter box-type frame, a ball joint front suspension (replacing kingpins), and an open driveshaft (replacing the enclosed torque tube). Eleven-inch drum brakes were used at each wheel, and the rear suspension was a strictly conventional leaf spring setup. Steering was also improved through the use of a recirculating-ball-type steering box.

Two engines were available: the 235ci Blue Flame inline six-cylinder rated at 123hp with a three-speed manual or a three-speed manual overdrive. Cars equipped with the optional Powerglide two-speed automatic transmission came with a Blue Flame six rated at 136hp. The overdrive transmission was made by Borg-Warner.

Most significant was the introduction of the optional Turbo-Fire small-block V-8 displacing 265ci. It was Chevrolet's first V-8 engine since 1917. It was available in two versions: a two-barrel rated at 162hp and a four-barrel rated at 180hp. The V-8 was optional on any 1955 Chevrolet model series. Overall, it was lighter than the six by about 41lb. It could be had with any transmission, but it did not come with an oil filter.

V-8–equipped Chevrolets could be identified by the use of a V-emblem and Chevrolet bow tie beneath each rear taillight, equidistant from the bumper top. A similar emblem was used on the steering wheel as well. Standard wheels measured 15x5in, and the standard tire size was 6.70x15.

A Bel Air convertible was chosen to be the pace car in the 1955 Indianapolis 500.

Things we take for granted today were optional in 1955—things such as turn signal indicators, back-up lights, outside rearview mirrors, and a heater and defroster. An outside rearview mirror was standard on the 1508 sedan delivery model, but it did not come with an inside rearview mirror.

Chevrolet listed the additional weight of the following options:

Oil filter	9.61lb
HD rear springs	19.31lb
Auxiliary seat	43lb
6.70x15 6-ply tires	13.45lb
Powerglide automatic	157.4lb
Overdrive	30lb
30/40amp Generator	28.81lb
Taxicab option	18.62lb
HD battery	10.78lb
Electric seat & window controls	31.97lb
Front stabilizer (police cars)	17.54lb
Power package (8cyl)	44.79lb
4bbl carburetor	17.7lb
Power brakes	15.57lb
AC	162.26lb

In addition, the use of the V-8 engine versus the six-cylinder resulted in a weight reduction of 26.57lb with the three-speed manual, 27.09lb with the overdrive, and 84.45lb with the Powerglide automatic.

1955 Bel Air Nomad

1955 Bel Air Sedan

*This 1955 Bel Air convertible was the official pace car for the
1955 Indianapolis 500. T.H. Keating, general manager of the
Chevrolet Motor Division, drove the pace car that year, and
Bob Sweikert won the race.*

1955 Bel Air Sport Coupe

1955 Bel Air Sport Coupe

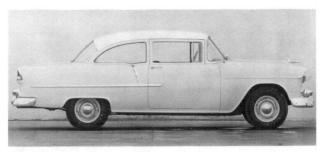

1955 Two-Ten Sedan

1955 One-Fifty Sedan

1955 Bel Air Sedan

1955 Two-Ten Sedan

Chapter 2

1956 Chevrolet

Production

Model	Number Built	Percentage of Total
150 Series, 6cyl & 8cyl		
1502 2dr sedan	82,735	5.09
1503 4dr sedan	55,333	3.40
1508 2dr sedan delivery	9,445	0.58
1512 2dr utility sedan	10,712	0.66
1529 2dr Handyman station wagon	13,739	0.84
Total	171,964	10.57
210 Series, 6cyl & 8cyl		
2102 2dr sedan	206,434	12.69
2103 4dr sedan	298,935	18.38
2109 4dr Townsman station wagon	114,646	7.05
2113 4dr hardtop sport sedan	21,131	1.30
2119 4dr Beauville station wagon	19,394	1.19
2124 2dr Delray club coupe	56,882	3.50
2129 2dr Handyman station wagon	22,381	1.38
2154 2dr hardtop sport coupe	19,079	1.17
Total	758,882	46.65
Bel Air Series, 6cyl & 8cyl		
2402 2dr sedan	105,098	6.46
2403 4dr sedan	282,476	17.36
2413 4dr hardtop sport sedan	109,261	6.71
2419 4dr Beauville station wagon	14,931	0.92
2429 2dr Nomad station wagon	8,103	0.50
2434 2dr convertible	41,883	2.57

2454 2dr hardtop sport		
coupe	130,778	8.04
Total	692,530	42.57

Corvette

2934 2dr convertible	3,467	0.21
Grand Total	1,626,843	100.00

Serial Numbers

Description

VC56F001001

V—V-8 engine (no letter *V*–6cyl engine)

C—Car series (A–150 Series, B–210 Series, C–Bel Air Series, D–sedan delivery series)

56—Last two digits of model year

F—Assembly plant (A–Atlanta, B–Baltimore, F–Flint, J–Janesville, K–Kansas City, L–Los Angeles, N–Norwood, O–Oakland, S–St. Louis, T–Tarrytown)

001001—Consecutive sequence number

Location

On stainless steel plate that is spot welded on left front door hinge post.

Basic Engine Specifications

(Horsepower/torque output)

235ci Blue Flame 6cyl—140 gross hp @ 4200rpm/210lb-ft @ 2400rpm; 125 net hp @ 4000rpm/195lb-ft @ 2000rpm

265ci Turbo-Fire 2bbl V-8—162 gross hp @ 4400rpm/257lb-ft @ 2200rpm; 137 net hp @ 4000rpm/235lb-ft @ 2200rpm

265ci Turbo-Fire 2bbl V-8—170 gross hp @ 4400rpm/257lb-ft @ 2200rpm; 141 net hp @ 4000rpm/235lb-ft @ 2200rpm

265ci Turbo-Fire 4bbl V-8—205 gross hp @ 4600rpm/268lb-ft @ 3000rpm; 170 net hp @ 4200rpm/240lb-ft @ 2800rpm

265ci Turbo-Fire 2x4bbl V-8—225 gross hp @ 5200rpm/270lb-ft @ 3600rpm; 196 net hp @ 4800rpm/250lb-ft @ 3400rpm

Engine and Transmission Suffix Codes

Z—235ci 6cyl 140hp, manual
ZC—235ci 6cyl 140hp, manual w/HD clutch
Y—235ci 6cyl 140hp, Powerglide automatic
G—265ci V-8 162hp, 3-speed
GC—265ci V-8 162hp, overdrive
GQ—265ci V-8 162hp, overdrive, AC
GE—265ci V-8 205hp, overdrive & 4bbl carburetor
GF—265ci V-8 162hp, 3-speed & AC
GJ—265ci V-8 162hp, HD clutch
GK—265ci V-8 162hp, 3-speed & AC
GS—265ci V-8 225hp, dual 4bbl carburetor
GT—265ci V-8 225hp, dual 4bbl carburetor & high-lift
    cam
F—265ci V-8 170hp, Powerglide
FC—265ci V-8 170hp, Powerglide & AC
GL—265ci V-8 205hp, 4bbl carburetor
GM—265ci V-8 205hp, 4bbl carburetor & AC
GN—265ci V-8 205hp, overdrive, 4bbl carburetor, & AC
FB—265ci V-8 205hp, Powerglide & 4bbl carburetor
FD—265ci V-8 205hp, Powerglide, 4bbl carburetor, &
    AC
FH—265ci V-8 225hp, Powerglide & dual 4bbl
    carburetor

Carburetors

235ci 6cyl, manual—7009255
235ci 6cyl, Powerglide—7009254
265ci V-8 162hp—7008387 (Manual transmission)
265ci V-8 170hp—7008388 (Powerglide transmission)
265ci V-8 205hp—Carter WCFB 2351S
265ci V-8 225hp—Carter WCFB 2419S front; 2362 rear

Distributors

235ci 6cyl—1112403
265ci 8cyl—1110847
265ci 8cyl 205hp—1110878

Coils

235ci 6cyl—1115085
265ci 8cyl—1115083

Generators
25amp 235ci—1100326
25amp 265ci—1100321
30amp 235/265ci—1102042
40amp (low–cut-in) 235/265ci—1106981

Regulators
25amp 235/265ci—1119000
30amp 235/265ci—1119001
40amp (low–cut-in) 235/265ci—1119004

Starting Motors
235ci 6cyl—1107644
265ci 8cyl—1107644

Option Order Codes (Including Factory D&H) and Retail Prices

Model	6cyl	8cyl
150 Series		
1502 2dr sedan	$1,797.00	$1,896.00
1503 4dr sedan	1,840.00	1,939.00
1512 2dr utility sedan	1,705.00	1,804.00
1529 2dr Handyman station wagon	2,142.00	2,241.00
210 Series		
2102 2dr sedan	1,883.00	1,982.00
2103 4dr sedan	1,926.00	2,025.00
2109 4dr Townsman station wagon	2,234.00	2,333.00
2113 4dr hardtop sport sedan	2,088.00	2,187.00
2119 4dr Beauville station wagon	2,319.00	2,418.00
2124 2dr Delray club coupe	1,942.00	2,041.00
2129 2dr Handyman station wagon	2,186.00	2,285.00
2154 2dr hardtop coupe	2,034.00	2,133.00
Bel Air Series		
2402 2dr sedan	1,996.00	2,095.00
2403 4dr sedan	2,039.00	2,138.00
2413 4dr hardtop sport sedan	2,201.00	2,300.00
2419 4dr Beauville station wagon	2,453.00	2,552.00
2429 2dr Nomad station wagon	2,579.00	2,678.00
2434 2dr convertible	2,315.00	2,414.00
2454 2dr hardtop sport coupe	2,147.00	2,246.00

Option Order Codes and Retail Prices

101	Heater (NA w/AC)	
	Airflow	$72.80
	Recirculating	48.15
104	Full-flow oil filter (V-8)	8.65
110	AC (incl. 30amp generator)	430.50
216	Oil bath air cleaner (6cyl only)	5.40
227	HD clutch	5.40
237	1-quart-capacity oil filter (6cyl)	8.65
241	Governor	
	6cyl	18.30
	V-8	43.05
254	HD rear springs	
	5-leaf	2.70
	Station wagon type	3.25
	6-leaf	
	1529, 2109, 2129	3.80
	1503, 2103, 2429	4.35
	All models	6.50
288	5 tires	
	6.70-15/6PRs	43.50
	6.70-16/6PR white sidewalls	86.55
290	5 6.70-15/4 white-sidewall tires	32.30
297	5 7.10-15/4PR tires	
	Wo/white sidewalls	13.25
	W/white sidewalls	48.75
313	Powerglide transmission	188.50
315	Overdrive transmission	107.60
320	Electric windshield wiper	11.35
324	Power steering	91.50
325	Generator	
	30amp	7.55
	40amp low–cut-in	7.55
345	HD battery (NA w/AC)	10.80
397	Electric seat controls (2100, 2400)	48.45
398	E-Z Eye glass	32.30
410	Super Turbo-Fire V-8 engine	32.30
411	Dual 4bbl carburetors (V-8)	242.10
412	Power brakes	37.70
417	Positive engine ventilation (6cyl)	12.95

426	Electric window controls	
	Except 2429, 2934	107.60
	2429, 2934	64.60
427	Padded instrument panel	16.15
449	High-lift camshaft equipment (V-8)	188.30
484–499	Trim combinations	6.00
500–523	Single colors	NC
525–558	Two-tone combinations	
	Standard	
	1500, 2100	12.95
	2400	25.85
	Special	
	2400	17.25
	2100	25.85

Dealer-installed Accessories and Retail Prices (Excluding Installation Charges)

Adapter—rear fender antenna	$3.50
Autotronic Eye	44.25
Belt—seat	10.95
Cap—locking gas	2.90
Carrier—Continental wheel	123.00
Clock—electric	17.65
Compass	5.95
Cover—seat, fiber	29.65
Cover—seat, nylon	42.50
Cover—seat, plastic	39.95
Covers—full wheel, set of 4	15.95
Covers—wheel disc, set of 4	19.00
Covers—wire wheel, set of 4	39.50
Dispenser—tissues	3.95
Extension—exhaust	3.25
Glareshade—windshield, 1	8.00
Guards—front fender & grille	39.80
Guard—rear fender	10.90
Guards—door edge, pair (sport coupe & convertible)	3.45
Guards—door edge, 4dr set	5.25
Harness—shoulder (used w/seatbelts)	9.50
Heater & defroster—deluxe	65.00
Heater & defroster—recirculating	42.00
Horn unit—vibrator	7.90

Dealer-installed Accessories and Retail Prices (Excluding Installation Charges)

Kool Kooshion	4.40
Lamp—luggage compartment	1.95
Lamp—underhood	1.95
Lamp—courtesy, pair	2.75
Lamp—back-up	6.25
Lamp—glove compartment	1.10
Mat units—floor, deluxe, 2	6.95
Mat unit—floor, rubber	3.50
Mirror—inside rearview, nonglare	4.50
Mirror—outside rearview, body mount	4.35
Mirror—outside rearview, remote control	6.95
Mirror—vanity visor	1.60
Molding—body sill	8.15
Molding—front fender top	5.85
Radio & antenna—push-button	85.00
Radio & antenna—manual	63.50
Radio & antenna—Signal Seeker	105.00
Raiser—automatic top	34.00
Safetylight & mirror	24.50
Screen—radiator insert	.95
Shields—door handle, set of 4	2.80
Shields—gravel, front fender, pair	6.95
Signal—parking brake, electric	4.25
Speaker—rear seat radio	12.00
Spotlight—hand, portable	7.95
Ventshades	8.75
Viewer—traffic light	2.90
Visor—outside	19.90
Washer—windshield, vacuum operated	7.95

One-Color Combinations
Chart split into two sections

Combination Number	Model Usage	Body Color
687	All models	Onyx Black
688	150 Series, 210 Series, 2402, 2403, 2413, 2419, 2434, 2454	Pinecrest Green

690	150 Series, 210 Series, 2402, 2403, 2413, 2434, 2454	Sherwood Green
691	150 Series, 210 Series, 2402, 2403, 2413, 2419, 2434, 2454	Nassau Blue
692	2102, 2103, 2113, 2154, 1508, 2402, 2403, 2413, 2434, 2454	Harbor Blue
693	2102, 2103, 2113, 2124, 2154, 2402, 2403, 2413	Dusk Plum
694	150 Series, 210 Series, 2102, 2103, 2113, 2124, 2154	India Ivory
695	150 Series (except 1508), 210 Series, 2102, 2103, 2113, 2124, 2154	Crocus Yellow
697	150 Series (except 1529), 210 Series, 2102, 2103, 2113, 2124, 2154	Matador Red
698	210 Series, 1502, 1503, 1512, 2102, 2103, 2113, 2124, 2154	Twilight Turquoise
749	150 Series (except 1508, 1529), 210	Tropical Turquoise

		Series, Bel Air (except 2429)	
750	150 Series (except 1508)		Calypso Cream
752	210 Series, Bel Air		Inca Silver

Combination Number	Model Usage	Wheel Color	Wheel Striping Color
687	All models	Black	Argent Silver
688	150 Series, 210 Series	Pinecrest Green	Onyx Black
688	2402, 2403, 2413, 2419, 2434, 2454	Pinecrest Green	None
690	150 Series, 210 Series	Sherwood Green	Argent Silver
690	2402, 2403, 2413, 2434, 2454	Sherwood Green	None
691	150 Series, 210 Series	Nassau Blue	Onyx Black
691	2402, 2403, 2413, 2419, 2434, 2454	Nassau Blue	None
692	2102, 2103, 2113, 2154, 1508	Harbor Blue	Argent Silver
692	2402, 2403, 2413, 2434, 2454	Harbor Blue	None
693	2102, 2103, 2113, 2124, 2154	Dusk Plum	Argent Silver
693	2402, 2403, 2413	Dusk Plum	None
694	150 Series, 210 Series	India Ivory	Onyx Black
694	2102, 2103, 2113, 2124, 2154	India Ivory	None
695	150 Series (except 1508), 210 Series	Crocus Yellow	Onyx Black
695	2102, 2103, 2113, 2124, 2154	Crocus Yellow	None
697	150 Series (except 1529), 210 Series	Matador Red	Onyx Black
697	2102, 2103, 2113, 2124, 2154	Matador Red	None

698	210 Series, 1502, 1503, 1512	Twilight Turquoise	Argent Silver
698	2102, 2103, 2113, 2124, 2154	Twilight Turquoise	None
749	150 Series (except 1508, 1529), 210 Series	Tropical Turquoise	Argent Silver
749	Bel Air (except 2429)	Tropical Turquoise	None
750	150 Series (except 1508)	Calypso Cream	Onyx Black
752	210 Series	Inca Silver	Onyx Black
752	Bel Air	Inca Silver	None

Two-Tone Color Combinations
Chart split into two sections

Combination Number	Model Usage	Upper/Lower Body Colors
696	150, 210, and Bel Air Series	Onyx Black/ Crocus Yellow
700	Bel Air Series	Adobe Beige/ Sierra Gold
701	150, 210, and Bel Air Series	India Ivory/ Onyx Black
702	150, 210, and Bel Air Series	Sherwood Green/ Pinecrest Green
703	2102, 2103, 2113, 2154, Bel Air Series (except 2419)	Harbor Blue/ Nassau Blue
705	150, 210, and Bel Air Series	India Ivory/ Pinecrest Green
706	150 and 210 Series, Bel Air Series (except 2419)	India Ivory/ Sherwood Green
707	150, 210, and Bel Air Series, 2454	India Ivory/ Nassau Blue
708	210 and Bel Air Series	India Ivory/ Dusk Plum
710	210 and Bel Air Series	India Ivory/ Twilight Turquoise

711	150 and 210 Series, 2402, 2403, 2434	India Ivory/ Matador Red
715	2413, 2419, 2429, 2454	Matador Red/ Dune Beige
717	210 and Bel Air Series	Crocus Yellow/ Laurel Green
721	210 Series (except 2124), Bel Air Series	India Ivory/ Dawn Gray
754	210 and Bel Air Series	India Ivory/ Tropical Turquoise
755	150 Series	Calypso Cream/ Onyx Black
756	150 and Bel Air Series, 210 Series (except 1508)	Grecian Gold/ Calypso Cream
757	210 and Bel Air Series	Inca Silver/ Imperial Ivory
763	2413, 2419, 2454	Matador Red/ Adobe Beige
792	210 and Bel Air Series	Crocus Yellow/ Laurel Green

Combination Number	Model Usage	Wheel Color	Wheel Striping Color
696	150 and 210 Series	Crocus Yellow	Onyx Black
696	Bel Air Series	Crocus Yellow	None
700	Bel Air Series	Sierra Gold	None
701	150 and 210 Series	Onyx Black	Argent Silver
701	Bel Air Series	Onyx Black	None
702	150 and 210 Series	Pinecrest Green	Onyx Black
702	Bel Air Series	Pinecrest Green	None
703	2102, 2103, 2113, 2154	Harbor Blue	Argent Silver
703	Bel Air Series (except 2419)	Harbor Blue	None
705	150 and 210 Series	Pinecrest Green	Onyx Black
705	Bel Air Series	Pinecrest Green	None
706	150 and 210 Series	Sherwood Green	Argent Silver

706	Bel Air Series (except 2419)	Sherwood Green	None
707	150 and 210 Series	Nassau Blue	Onyx Black
707	Bel Air Series, 2454	Nassau Blue	None
708	210 Series	Dusk Plum	Argent Silver
708	Bel Air Series	Dusk Plum	None
710	210 Series	Twilight Turquoise	Argent Silver
710	Bel Air Series	Twilight Turquoise	None
711	150 and 210 Series	Matador Red	Onyx Black
711	2402, 2403, 2434	Matador Red	None
715	2413, 2419, 2429, 2454	Matador Red	None
717	210 Series	Laurel Green	Argent Silver
717	Bel Air Series	Laurel Green	None
721	210 Series (except 2124)	Dawn Gray	Onyx Black
721	Bel Air Series	Dawn Gray	None
754	210 Series	Tropical Turquoise	Argent Silver
754	Bel Air Series	Tropical Turquoise	None
755	150 Series	Calypso Cream	Onyx Black
756	150 and 210 Series (except 1508)	Grecian Gold	Onyx Black
756	Bel Air Series	Grecian Gold	None
757	210 Series	Imperial Ivory	Onyx Black
757	Bel Air Series	Imperial Ivory	None
763	2413, 2419, 2454	Matador Red	None
792	210 and Bel Air Series	Laurel Green	None

Interior Trim Combinations

- 560 Gold dotted black cloth—gold striped imitation leather
- 562 Medium green—gold striped imitation leather
- 564 Charcoal pattern cloth—Starfrost
- 565 Green pattern cloth—Starfrost
- 566 Blue pattern cloth—Starfrost
- 567 Black—ivory imitation leather
- 568 Green—ivory imitation leather
- 569 Turquoise—ivory imitation leather
- 570 Medium green imitation leather—Starfrost
- 572 Medium turquoise imitation leather—Starfrost
- 573 Charcoal pattern cloth—ivory imitation leather

Interior Trim Combinations

574 Green pattern cloth—green imitation leather
575 Blue pattern cloth—blue imitation leather
577 Turquoise pattern cloth—turquoise imitation leather
578 Charcoal pattern cloth—yellow imitation leather
579 Charcoal pattern cloth—ivory imitation leather
580 Medium green pattern cloth—light green imitation leather
581 Medium blue pattern cloth—light blue imitation leather
584 Medium turquoise pattern cloth—light turquoise imitation leather
585 Charcoal pattern cloth—yellow imitation leather
587 Medium turquoise pattern cloth—light turquoise imitation leather
588 Charcoal pattern cloth—yellow imitation leather
590 Medium green pattern cloth—light green imitation leather
591 Light blue pattern cloth—light blue imitation leather
593 Red pattern cloth—red imitation leather
594 Medium turquoise pattern cloth—light turquoise imitation leather
595 Charcoal pattern cloth—yellow imitation leather
602 Charcoal—ivory imitation leather
603 Turquoise—ivory imitation leather
604 Charcoal—yellow imitation leather
605 Red—ivory imitation leather
606 Medium green—light green imitation leather
607 Medium blue—light blue imitation leather
609 Charcoal imitation leather—Starfrost
610 Charcoal pattern cloth—ivory imitation leather
611 Charcoal pattern cloth—ivory imitation leather
615 Charcoal gray—gold striped imitation leather
616 Charcoal gray—gold striped imitation leather
617 Copper pattern cloth—tan imitation leather
618 Tan pattern cloth—copper imitation leather
619 Tan pattern cloth—copper imitation leather
620 Tan pattern cloth—copper imitation leather
621 Copper—tan imitation leather
626 Charcoal pattern cloth—cream imitation leather

627	Charcoal-&-yellow pattern cloth—cream imitation leather
628	Red-&-taupe pattern cloth—red imitation leather
629	Red-&-taupe pattern cloth—red imitation leather
630	Charcoal-&-yellow pattern cloth—cream imitation leather
631	Charcoal imitation leather—cream imitation leather
632	Charcoal-&-yellow pattern cloth—cream imitation leather
633	Red-&-taupe pattern cloth—red imitation leather

Exterior Color and Interior Trim Combinations

Note: Parentheses indicate optional custom colored interior.

150 Series

	Interior Trim	
Exterior Color	**1502, 1503, 1512**	**1529**
687 Onyx Black	560	616
688 Pinecrest Green	560	562
690 Sherwood Green	560	562
691 Nassau Blue	560	616
694 India Ivory	560	616
695 Crocus Yellow	560	616
696 Onyx Black/Crocus Yellow	560	616
697 Matador Red	560	—
698 Twilight Turquoise	560	—
701 India Ivory/Onyx Black	560	616
702 Sherwood Green/ Pinecrest Green	560	562
705 India Ivory/Pinecrest Green	560	562
706 India Ivory/Sherwood Green	—	562
707 India Ivory/Nassau Blue	560	616
711 India Ivory/Matador Red	560	—
755 Calypso Cream/Onyx Black	560	616
756 Grecian Gold/Calypso Cream	560	616

210 Series · Interior Trim

Exterior Color	2102, 2103, 2113, 2154	2124	2109, 2119, 2129
687 Onyx Black	564	567	609
688 Pinecrest Green	564 (565)	567 (568)	609 (570)
690 Sherwood Green	564 (565)	567 (568)	609 (570)
691 Nassau Blue	564 (566)	567	609
692 Harbor Blue	564 (566)	567	—
693 Dusk Plum	564	567	—
694 India Ivory	564	567	609
695 Crocus Yellow	564	567	609
696 Onyx Black/ Crocus Yellow	564	567	609
697 Matador Red	564	567	609
698 Twilight Turquoise	564	567 (569)	609 (572)
701 India Ivory/ Onyx Black	564	567	609
702 Sherwood Green/ Pinecrest Green	564 (565)	567	609
703 Harbor Blue/ Nassau Blue	564 (566)	—	—
705 India Ivory/ Pinecrest Green	564 (565)	567 (568)	609 (570)
706 India Ivory/ Sherwood Green	564 (565)	567 (568)	609 (570)
707 India Ivory/ Nassau Blue	564 (566)	567	609
708 India Ivory/ Dusk Plum	564	567	609
711 India Ivory/ Matador Red	564	567	609
717 Crocus Yellow/ Laurel Green	564	567	609
721 India Ivory/ Dawn Gray	564	—	609
754 India Ivory/ Tropical Turquoise	564	567	609
756 Grecian Gold/ Calypso Cream	564	567	609
757 Inca Silver/ Imperial White	564	567	609

Bel Air Series

Exterior	Interior Trim		
Color	2402, 2403	2413	2419
687 Onyx Black	573(578)	579(585)	610(588)
688 Pinecrest Green	573(574)	579(580)	610
690 Sherwood Green	573(574)	579(580)	—
691 Nassau Blue	573(575)	579(580)	610
692 Harbor Blue	573(575)	579(581)	—
693 Dusk Plum	573	579	610
694 India Ivory	573	579	610
695 Crocus Yellow	573(578)	579(585)	610(588)
696 Onyx Black/ Crocus Yellow	573(577)	579(585)	610(588)
697 Matador Red	573	579(628)	610(629)
698 Twilight Turquoise	573(577)	579(584)	610(587)
700 Adobe Beige/Sierra Gold	617	618	619
701 India Ivory/ Onyx Black	573	579	610
702 Sherwood Green/ Pinecrest Green	573(574)	579(580)	—
703 Harbor Blue/ Nassau Blue	573(575)	579(581)	—
705 India Ivory/ Pinecrest Green	573(574)	579(580)	610

45

	Interior Trim		
Exterior Color	**2402, 2403**	**2413**	**2419**
706 India Ivory/ Sherwood Green	573(574)	579(580)	—
707 India Ivory/ Nassau Blue	573(575)	579(581)	610
708 India Ivory/ Dusk Plum	573	579	610
710 India Ivory/ Twilight Turquoise	573(577)	579(584)	610(587)
711 India Ivory/ Matador Red	573	—	—
715 Matador Red/Dune Beige	—	579(628)	610(629)
717 Crocus Yellow/ Laurel Green	573(577)	579(585)	610(588)
721 India Ivory/ Dawn Gray	573	579	610
754 India Ivory/ Tropical Turquoise	573	579	610
756 Grecian Gold/ Calypso Cream	617	618	619
757 Inca Silver/ Imperial Ivory	573	574	610

Exterior Color			
763 Matador Red/ Adobe Beige	579(628)	610(629)	—

Interior Trim

Exterior Color	2429	2434	2454
687 Onyx Black	611(595)	602(604)	579(585)
688 Pinecrest Green	—	602(606)	579(580)
690 Sherwood Green	—	602(606)	579(580)
691 Nassau Blue	—	602(607)	579(581)
692 Harbor Blue	—	602(607)	579(581)
693 Dusk Plum	—	602	579
694 India Ivory	—	602	579
695 Crocus Yellow	—	602(604)	579(585)
696 Onyx Black/ Crocus Yellow	611(595)	602(604)	579
697 Matador Red	—	602(605)	579(628)
698 Twilight Turquoise	—	602(603)	579(584)
700 Adobe Beige/ Sierra Gold	620	621	618
701 India Ivory/ Onyx Black	611	602	579
702 Sherwood Green/ Pinecrest Green	611(590)	—	579(580)
703 Harbor Blue/Nassau Blue	611(591)	602(607)	579(581)

Exterior Color	Interior Trim		
	2429	2434	2454
705 India Ivory/ Pinecrest Green	611(590)	602(606)	579(580)
706 India Ivory/ Sherwood Green	611(590)	602(606)	579(580)
707 India Ivory/ Nassau Blue	611(591)	602(607)	579(581)
708 India Ivory/ Dusk Plum	611	602	579
710 India Ivory/ Twilight Turquoise	611(594)	602(603)	579
711 India Ivory/ Matador Red	—	602(605)	579
715 Matador Red/Dune Beige	—	—	—
717 Crocus Yellow/ Laurel Green	611	602(604)	579(585)
721 India Ivory/ Dawn Gray	611	602	579
754 India Ivory/ Tropical Turquoise	611	602	579
756 Grecian Gold/ Calypso Cream	620	621	618

| 757 Inca Silver/ Imperial Ivory | 611 | 602 | 579 |
| 763 Matador Red/Adobe Beige | — | — | — |

Note: Parentheses indicate optional custom colored interior.

Convertible Top Colors
Ivory
Black
Tan
Light blue

Facts

The Chevrolet passenger cars received a minor facelift for 1956. Most noticeable was a full-width front grille and a longer, flatter hood. The hood also had a pronounced V-treatment. The hood ornament was redesigned, and a large Chevrolet emblem was located in the front center of the hood. On V-8–equipped cars, a large chromed *V* was located beneath the Chevrolet emblem. The same treatment was repeated on the rear deck. The side treatment also differed on the 1956, primarily on the wheel openings, which were elongated and flared and designed to accentuate a longer, lower look. In the rear, redesigned taillights were the most obvious change and the left taillight assembly hid the fuel filler cap. Chevrolet script was used on the rear fenders on the 150s and 210s, and Bel Air script and a Chevrolet emblem were used on the Bel Airs. Overall, the 1956 models were longer by 2in—3in on the station wagons.

The bottom of the line was represented by the 150 Series. It was offered in two- and four-door sedans, a two-door utility sedan, a two-door Handyman station wagon, and a two-door sedan delivery, which could be had with 150 Series trim. Some effort was made to spruce up the 150 Series' Spartan image with the use of gold vinyl trim and gold dotted upholstery. On the exterior, bright trim was used around the windshield and rear window and a stainless steel molding that ran from the front fender, along the side of the car, to a vertical molding that originated at the beltline notch made it possible for the 150 Series to use more elaborate two-tone paint. Even so, the 150s were bare-bones cars, as they came with only a single driver's-side visor and lacked coat hooks, armrests, ashtrays, and padded seats.

The 210 model designation was expanded and used on eight body styles: two- and four-door sedans; a two-door Delray club coupe; a two-door sport coupe; a four-door sport sedan; a two-door Handyman station wagon; a four-door, six-passenger Townsman station wagon; and a nine-passenger Beauville station wagon. The four-door sport sedan differed from the regular four-door sedan in that it did not have center window pillars. In the interior, the 210s got new upholstery materials: a charcoal gray nylon-faced pattern cloth with Starfrost vinyl, except for the club coupe, which got an all-vinyl interior. Optional were custom colored interiors, which were keyed to the exterior colors. On the exterior, the 210s got a side molding that extended rearward from the front fender and sloped downward as it approached the rear bumper. A sash molding ran down from the beltline notch to meet this side molding. As in 1955, the 210s came with more standard interior features.

The Bel Airs were available in seven different body styles: two- and four-door sedans, a two-door sport coupe, a four-door sport sedan, a convertible, a two-door Nomad wagon, and a four-door Beauville station wagon, which came with a third rear seat for nine-passenger capacity. As in 1955, the Bel Airs came with more standard features such as carpeting and an electric clock. Their exterior side treatment followed the pattern of the 210s but was highlighted by the use of an additional upper molding that originated at the rear sash molding and met the lower molding at the front fender in a V. The Bel Airs came with full wheel covers.

The Nomad two-door wagon continued in 1956 but without its special interior, front eyebrow moldings, and unique wheel cutouts. The angle of the rear quarter panel sash molding differed on the Nomad, corresponding with the angle on the B-pillar. Another difference on the Nomad was the use of V-emblems beneath the taillights to signify a V-8. These were similar to but not interchangeable with the ones used on the 1955 cars.

Engine and transmission availability was the same as in 1955, but horsepower ratings were higher. The 235ci Blue Flame six was rated at 140hp thanks to a higher-lift camshaft that actuated hydraulic lifters and a higher compression ratio of 8:1. The Turbo-Fire 265ci V-8 was rated at 162hp for use with the manual three-speed and overdrive transmissions. Powerglide-equipped cars got a 265ci V-8 that had a higher-lift camshaft and generated 170hp. Optional was the Super Turbo-Fire 265ci V-8, which came with a higher-lift camshaft, a 9.25:1 compression ratio, and a four-barrel carburetor with dual exhausts, for a 205hp rating. Also optional was a dual four-barrel setup for 225hp. A three-finger clutch pressure plate was used on all Super Turbo-Fire engines.

Several mechanical improvements were made for 1956. All V-8s came with a full-flow oil filter. The generator was mounted differently to reduce vibration, the voltage regulator was made waterproof, and turn signal indicators were made standard equipment. A larger 53amp-hr battery was also standard equipment.

Through the use of a revised tailpipe design and hangers, dual exhausts were installed on station wagons and sedan deliverys when the Super Turbo-Fire engine was specified.

1956 150 Two-Door Sedan

The dual four-barrel intake setup came with an aluminum intake manifold.

Seatbelts and shoulder harnesses were optional as dealer-installed accessories for the first time. Another safety-related option was the padded dash.

Standard wheels measured 15x5in with 6.70x15 tires. Optional were 7.10x15 four-ply tires.

1956 Bel Air Sport Sedan

1956 Two-Ten Sport Coupe

1956 Bel Air Sedan

1956 One-Fifty Sedan

1956 Two-Ten Sedan

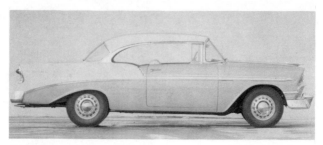

1956 Bel Air Sport Coupe

1956 Bel Air Sport Sedan

Chapter 3

1957 Chevrolet

Production

Model	Number Built	Percentage of Total
150 Series, 6cyl & 8cyl		
1502 2dr sedan	71,135	4.55
1503 4dr sedan	56,418	3.61
1508 2dr sedan delivery	8,907	0.57
1512 2dr utility sedan	8,817	0.56
1529 2dr Handyman station wagon	15,087	0.97
Total	160,364	10.26
210 Series, 6cyl & 8cyl		
2102 2dr sedan	162,851	10.43
2103 4dr sedan	273,696	17.53
2109 4dr Townsman station wagon	128,941	8.26
2113 4dr hardtop sport sedan	18,206	1.16
2119 4dr Beauville station wagon	23,862	1.53
2124 2dr Delray club coupe	25,952	1.66
2129 2dr Handyman station wagon	17,996	1.15
2154 2dr hardtop sport coupe	23,092	1.48
Total	674,596	43.20
Bel Air Series, 6cyl & 8cyl		
2402 2dr sedan	62,942	4.03
2403 4dr sedan	264,449	16.93
2409 4dr Beauville station wagon	27,822	1.78
2413 4dr hardtop sport sedan	142,518	9.13
2429 2dr Nomad station wagon	6,264	0.40

Model	Number Built	Percentage of Total
2434 2dr convertible	48,068	3.08
2454 2dr hardtop sport coupe	168,293	10.78
Total	720,356	46.13
Corvette		
2934 2dr convertible	6,339	0.41
Grand Total	1,561,655	100.00

Serial Numbers

Description
VC57F100001

V—V-8 engine (no letter V–6cyl engine)

C—Car series (A–150 Series, B–210 Series, C–Bel Air Series, D–sedan delivery series)

57—Last two digits of model year

F—Assembly plant (A–Atlanta, B–Baltimore, F–Flint, J–Janesville, K–Kansas City, L–Los Angeles, N–Norwood, O–Oakland, S–St. Louis, T–Tarrytown)

100001—Consecutive sequence number

Location
On stainless steel plate that is spot welded on left front door hinge post.

Basic Engine Specifications
(Horsepower/torque output)

235ci Blue Flame 1bbl 6cyl—140 gross hp @ 4200rpm/210lb-ft @ 2400rpm; 125 net hp @ 4000rpm/195lb-ft @ 2000rpm

265ci Turbo-Fire 2bbl V-8—162 gross hp @ 4400rpm/257lb-ft @ 2200rpm; 137 net hp @ 4000rpm/235lb-ft @ 2200rpm

283ci Super Turbo-Fire 2bbl V-8—185 gross hp @ 4600rpm/275lb-ft @ 2400rpm; 150 net hp @ 4200rpm/245lb-ft @ 2400–2800rpm

283ci Turbo-Fire 4bbl V-8—220 gross hp @ 4800rpm/300lb-ft @ 3000rpm; 190 net hp @ 4600rpm/270lb-ft @ 2800rpm

283ci Turbo-Fire 2x4bbl V-8—245 gross hp @ 5000rpm/300lb-ft @ 3800rpm; 215 net hp @ 4800rpm/270lb-ft @ 3400rpm

283ci Turbo-Fire 2x4bbl V-8—270 gross hp @
6000rpm/285lb-ft @ 4200rpm; 230 net hp @
6000rpm/255lb-ft @ 3800rpm
283ci Turbo-Fire FI V-8—250 gross hp @
5000rpm/305lb-ft @ 3800rpm; 225 net hp @
4800rpm/280lb-ft @ 3400rpm
283ci Turbo-Fire FI V-8—283 gross hp @
6200rpm/290lb-ft @ 4400rpm; 240 net hp @
5600rpm/265lb-ft @ 4200rpm

Engine and Transmission Suffix Codes

A—235ci 6cyl 140hp, manual
AD—235ci 6cyl 140hp, HD clutch
B—235ci 6cyl 140hp, Powerglide automatic
C—265ci V-8 162hp, 3-speed
CD—265ci V-8 162hp, overdrive
CE—265ci V-8 162hp, HD clutch
E—283ci V-8 220hp, 4bbl carburetor
EA—283ci V-8 245hp, dual 4bbl carburetor
EB—283ci V-8 270hp, dual 4bbl carburetor & high-lift
cam
EC—283ci V-8 220hp, overdrive & 4bbl carburetor
FC—283ci V-8 220hp, Powerglide & 4bbl carburetor
FD—283ci V-8 245hp, Powerglide & dual 4bbl
carburetor
FA—283ci V-8 185hp, Powerglide & AC
FE—283ci V-8 220hp, Powerglide, AC, & 4bbl
carburetor
FJ—283ci V-8 250hp, Powerglide & FI
G—283ci V-8 185hp, Turboglide
GC—283ci V-8 220hp, Turboglide & 4bbl carburetor
GD—283ci V-8 245hp, Turboglide & dual 4bbl
carburetor
GF—283ci V-8 250hp, Turboglide & FI
EJ—283ci V-8 250hp, FI
EK—283ci V-8 283hp, FI & high-lift cam

Carburetors

235ci 6cyl, manual—7009657
235ci 6cyl, Powerglide—7009656
265ci V-8 162hp—7011131
283ci V-8 170hp—7011224
283ci V-8 245/270hp—3730599 front; 3720953 rear

Distributors
235ci 6cyl—1112403
265ci V-8—1110874
283ci V-8 170hp—1110874
283ci V-8 220hp—1110890
283ci V-8 245/270hp—1110891
283ci V-8 250/283hp—1110891

Coils
235ci 6cyl—1115085
265/283ci V-8—1115083

Generators
25amp 235ci—1100326
25amp 235/265/283ci—1100321
30amp 235/265/283ci—1102042
40amp (low–cut-in) 235/265/283ci—1106981

Regulators
25amp—1119000
FI—1110906; 1110905 w/high-lift camshaft

Starting Motors
235ci 6cyl—1107652
265ci 8cyl—1107664
283ci 8cyl, manual or Powerglide—1107644
283ci 8cyl, Turboglide—1107694

Option Order Codes (Including Factory D&H) and Retail Prices

Model	6cyl	8cyl
150 Series		
1502 2dr sedan	$1,956.32	$2,056.32
1503 4dr sedan	2,008.32	2,108.32
1512 2dr utility sedan	1,845.32	1,945.32
1529 2dr Handyman station wagon	2,267.32	2,367.32
210 Series		
2102 2dr sedan	2,082.32	2,182.32
2103 4dr sedan	2,134.32	2,234.32
2109 4dr station wagon	2,416.32	2,516.32

2113 4dr sport sedan	2,230.32	2,330.32
2119 4dr station wagon	2,523.32	2,623.32
2124 2dr Delray coupe	2,122.32	2,222.32
2129 2dr station wagon	2,362.32	2,462.32
2154 2dr sport coupe	2,164.32	2,264.32

Bel Air Series

2402 2dr sedan	2,198.32	2,298.32
2403 4dr sedan	2,250.32	2,350.32
2409 4dr station wagon	2,540.32	2,640.32
2413 4dr sport sedan	2,324.32	2,424.32
2429 2dr Nomad station wagon	2,717.32	2,817.32
2434 2dr convertible	2,471.32	2,571.32
2454 2dr sport coupe	2,259.32	2,359.32

Option Order Codes and Retail Prices

101	Heater (NA w/AC)	
	Airflow	$74.90
	Recirculating	48.15
104	Full-flow oil filter (V-8)	8.65
110–111	AC (incl. 30amp generator)	430.40
216	Oil bath air cleaner (6cyl only)	5.40
227	HD clutch	5.40
237	1-quart-capacity oil filter (6cyl)	8.65
241	Governor	
	6cyl	18.30
	V-8	37.70
254	HD rear springs	
	5-leaf (except wagons)	2.70
	Station wagon type	3.25
	6-leaf	
	1529, 2109, 2129, 2429	3.80
	2429, 2434	4.35
	Except wagons	6.50
303	Close-ratio transmission	59.20
313	Powerglide transmission	188.30
315	Overdrive transmission	107.60
320	Electric windshield wiper	11.30
324	Power steering	69.95
325	Generator	
	35amp	7.55
	40amp low–cut-in	80.70

345	HD battery (NA w/AC)	7.55
397	Electric seat controls (2100, 2400)	43.05
398	E-Z Eye glass	32.30
410	Super Turbo-Fire V-8 engine	43.05
411	Dual 4bbl carburetors (V-8)	
	Wo/high-lift camshaft	209.85
	W/high-lift camshaft	242.10
412	Power brakes	37.70
417	Positive engine ventilation (6cyl)	12.95
426	Electric window controls	
	2100–2400, except 2329	102.25
	2429, 2934	59.20
427	Padded instrument panel	16.15
465	5 tires	
	7.50-14/4PR white sidewalls, (except 2119)	31.60
	7.50-14/6PRs	42.85
466	5 white-sidewall tires	
	7.50-14/6s (except 2119)	85.00
	7.50-14/6PRs (2119)	42.85
480–499	Trim combinations	NC
500–524	Single colors	NC
525–559	Two-tone combinations (1500, 2100, 2400)	21.55
578	FI equipment	550.00
675	3.36:1-ratio limited-slip differential	45.00
676	3.55:1-ratio limited-slip differential	45.00
678	4.11:1-ratio limited-slip differential	45.00

Dealer-installed Accessories and Retail Prices (Excluding Installation Charges)

Antenna—electric, RH rear fender	$28.75
Antenna—manual, RH front	6.35
Antenna—manual, LH rear	9.80
Antenna—dummy, RH rear fender	6.95
Autotronic Eye	44.25
Belt—seat	10.95
Cap—locking gasoline tank	3.25
Carrier—Continental wheel	129.50
Clock—electric	17.85
Compass—illuminated	5.95
Cover—accelerator pedal	1.30

Covers—full wheel, set of 4	21.45
Cushion—bumper, rubber	3.90
Dispenser—tissues	4.40
Filter unit—gasoline	2.45
Frame—license	4.25
Frame—license, gold	6.95
Glareshade—windshield, 1	7.25
Guards—bumper, front & rear, set	27.50
Guards—door edge, pair (sport coupe & convertible)	3.45
Guards—door edge, 4dr	6.25
Harness—shoulder (used w/seatbelts)	9.50
Horn unit—3rd note	8.75
Kit—tool	3.55
Kool Kooshion—blue, green, tan	4.55
Kool Kooshion—black & ivory	5.20
Lamp—luggage compartment	2.10
Lamp—underhood	2.10
Lamp—courtesy, pair	2.75
Lamp—back-up	12.00
Lamp—glove compartment	1.15
Lighter—cigarette	3.35
Litter container	2.95
Mat units—floor, deluxe, 2	6.95
Mat unit—floor, rubber	3.80
Mirror—inside rearview, nonglare	4.95
Mirror—outside rearview, body mount	4.40
Mirror—outside rearview, deluxe w/ring	5.95
Mirror—vanity visor	1.60
Molding—body sill	8.35
Molding—trunk lid, lower edge	11.60
Radio & antenna—manual	65.50
Radio & antenna—push-button	89.50
Radio & antenna—Wonder Bar	112.00
Radio & LH rear antenna—manual	65.50
Radio & LH rear antenna—push-button	89.50
Radio & LH rear antenna—Wonder Bar	112.00
Rest—arm, pair	9.90
Safetylight & mirror	24.50
Screen—radiator insert	.95
Shaver—electric AC/DC 12-volt	31.50
Shields—door handle, set of 4	3.25

Dealer-installed Accessories and Retail Prices (Excluding Installation Charges)

Signal—parking brake, electric	4.85
Speaker—rear seat radio	12.25
Spinners—wheel, set	9.85
Spotlight—hand, portable	7.95
Tank—vacuum	5.40
Tray—vacuum, ash	9.95
Ventshades	9.75
Viewer—traffic light	2.95
Visor—outside	19.95
Washer—windshield, push-button	10.65
Washer—windshield, foot operated	7.95

One-Color Combinations

Combination	Model Usage	Body Color	Wheel Color
793	All models	Onyx Black	Black
794	150 Series (except 1529), 210 Series, Bel Air Series (except 2409–2429)	Imperial Ivory	Imperial Ivory
795	All models	Larkspur Blue	Larkspur Blue
796	All models	Harbor Blue	Harbor Blue
797	All models	Surf Green	Surf Green
798	All models	Highland Green	Highland Green
799	150 Series (except 1508), 210 Series, Bel Air Series	Tropical Turquoise	Tropical Turquoise
800	150 Series (except 1508), 210 Series, Bel Air Series	Colonial Cream	Colonial Cream
801	Bel Air convertible (2434)	Canyon Coral	Canyon Coral

802	All models	Matador Red	Matador Red
803	Bel Air convertible (2434)	Coronado Yellow	Coronado Yellow
804	210 Series, Bel Air Series	Inca Silver	Inca Silver
805	2104, 2109, 2119, 2129, Bel Air Series	Sierra Gold	Sierra Gold
806	150 Series (except 1508), 210 Series, Bel Air Series	Adobe Beige	Adobe Beige
821	Bel Air convertible (2434)	Dusk Pearl	Dusk Pearl
823	Bel Air convertible (2434)	Laurel Green	Laurel Green

Two-Tone Color Combinations

Combi-nation	Model Usage	Upper/Lower Body Colors	Wheel Color
807	150 Series (except 1508), 210 Series, Bel Air Series (except 2434)	India Ivory/ Onyx Black	Black
808	150 Series (except 1508), 210 Series, Bel Air Series (except 2434)	Imperial Ivory/Inca Silver	Inca Silver

Combi-nation	Model Usage	Upper/Lower Body Colors	Wheel Color
809	150 Series (except 1508), Bel Air Series (except 2434)	Larkspur Blue/ Harbor Blue	Harbor Blue
	210 Series	Harbor Blue/ Larkspur Blue	Larkspur Blue
810	150 Series (except 1508), 210 Series, Bel Air Series (except 2434)	India Ivory/ Larkspur Blue	Larkspur Blue
811	150 Series (except 1508), 210 Series, Bel Air Series (except 2434)	India Ivory/ Tropical Turquoise	Tropical Turquoise
812	150 Series (except 1508)	Surf Green	Surf Green
	210 Series	Surf Green/ Highland Green	Surf Green
	Bel Air Series (except 2434)	Surf Green/ Highland Green	Highland Green
813	150 Series (except 1508), 210 Series, Bel Air Series (except 2434)	India Ivory/ Surf Green	Surf Green

814	210 Series, Bel Air Series (except 2434)	India Ivory/ Coronado Yellow	Coronado Yellow
815	150 Series (except 1508), Bel Air Series (except 2434)	Colonial Cream	Colonial Cream
	210 Series	Colonial Cream/ Onyx Black	Black
816	150 Series (except 1508), Bel Air Series (except 2434)	Colonial Cream	Colonial Cream
	210 Series	Colonial Cream/ India Ivory	Colonial Cream
817	210 Series, Bel Air Series (except 2434)	India Ivory/ Canyon Coral	Canyon Coral
818	2124, 2109, 2119, 2129, Bel Air Series (except 2434)	Adobe Beige/ Sierra Gold	Sierra Gold
819	150 Series (except 1508), 210 Series, Bel Air Series (except 2434)	India Ivory/ Matador Red	Matador Red

Combi-nation	Model Usage	Upper/Lower Body Colors	Wheel Color
820	210 Series	Colonial Cream/ Laurel Green	Colonial Cream
	Bel Air Series (except 2434)	Laurel Green	Laurel Green
822	210 Series	Dusk Pearl/ Imperial Ivory	Dusk Pearl
	Bel Air Series (except 2434)	Dusk Pearl	Dusk Pearl

Interior Trim Combinations

650 Black & gray cloth—black imitation leather
651 Black & gray imitation leather—black imitation leather
652 Black & gray imitation leather—black imitation leather
653 Green & gray imitation leather—metallic medium green imitation leather
654 Charcoal cloth—ivory imitation leather
655 Medium green cloth—light green imitation leather
656 Medium blue cloth—light blue imitation leather
657 Charcoal imitation leather—ivory imitation leather
658 Metallic medium green imitation leather—light green imitation leather
659 Beige imitation leather—metallic copper imitation leather
660 Charcoal imitation leather—ivory imitation leather
661 Metallic medium green imitation leather—light green imitation leather
662 Metallic copper imitation leather—beige imitation leather
663 Black & silver cloth—silver imitation leather

664 Black & green cloth—metallic medium green imitation leather

665 Black & blue cloth—medium blue imitation leather

666 Black & turquoise cloth—medium turquoise imitation leather

667 Black & copper cloth—beige imitation leather

668 Black & yellow cloth—yellow imitation leather

669 Black & red cloth—red imitation leather

670 Black & silver cloth—silver imitation leather

671 Black & dark green pattern cloth—metallic medium green imitation leather

672 Black & dark blue cloth—medium blue imitation leather

673 Black & dark turquoise cloth—medium turquoise imitation leather

674 Black & copper cloth—beige imitation leather

675 Black & yellow cloth—yellow imitation leather

676 Black & red cloth—red imitation leather

677 Metallic silver imitation leather—ivory imitation leather

678 Metallic medium green imitation leather—light green imitation leather

679 Medium blue imitation leather—light blue imitation leather

680 Medium turquoise imitation leather—ivory imitation leather

681 Metallic copper imitation leather—beige imitation leather

682 Metallic silver imitation leather—yellow imitation leather

683 Metallic silver imitation leather—red imitation leather

684 Black & silver cloth—metallic silver imitation leather

685 Black & dark green cloth—metallic medium green imitation leather

686 Black & dark blue cloth—medium blue imitation leather

687 Black & dark turquoise cloth—medium turquoise imitation leather

688 Black & copper cloth—beige imitation leather

Interior Trim Combinations

689 Black & yellow cloth—yellow imitation leather
690 Black & red cloth—red imitation leather
691 Black & silver cloth—silver imitation leather
692 Black & dark green cloth—medium green
       imitation leather
693 Black & dark blue cloth—medium blue imitation
       leather
694 Black & dark turquoise cloth—medium
       turquoise imitation leather
695 Black & copper cloth—beige imitation leather
696 Black & yellow cloth—yellow imitation leather
697 Black & red cloth—red imitation leather

Exterior Color and Interior Trim Combinations

150 Series

| | Interior Trim | | |
Exterior Color	1502, 1503, 1512	1529	1508
793 Onyx Black	650	652	651
794 Imperial Ivory	650	652	651
795 Larkspur Blue	650	652	651
796 Harbor Blue	650	652	651
797 Surf Green	650	652	651
798 Highland Green	650	652	651
799 Tropical Turquoise	650	652	—
800 Colonial Cream	650	652	—
802 Matador Red	650	652	651
806 Adobe Beige	650	652	—
807 India Ivory/Onyx Black	650	652	—
808 Imperial Ivory/Inca Silver	650	652	—
809 Larkspur Blue/Harbor Blue	650	652	—
810 India Ivory/Larkspur Blue	650	652	—
811 India Ivory/Tropical Turquoise	650	652	—
812 Surf Green/Highland Green	650	652	—
813 India Ivory/Surf Green	650	652	—

815 Colonial Cream	650	652	—
816 Colonial Cream/India Ivory	650	652	—
819 India Ivory/Matador Red	650	652	—

210 Series

	Interior Trim		
Exterior Color	**2102, 2103, 2113, 2154**	**2124**	**2109, 2119, 2129**
793 Onyx Black	654	657	660
794 Imperial Ivory	654	657	660
795 Larkspur Blue	656	657	660
796 Harbor Blue	656	657	660
797 Surf Green	655	661	658
798 Highland Green	655	661	658
799 Tropical Turquoise	654	657	660
800 Colonial Cream	654	657	660
802 Matador Red	654	657	660
804 Inca Silver	654	657	660
805 Sierra Gold	—	659	662
806 Adobe Beige	654	659	662
807 India Ivory/Onyx Black	654	657	660
808 Imperial Ivory/Inca Silver	654	657	660
809 Larkspur Blue/Harbor Blue	656	657	660
810 India Ivory/Larkspur Blue	656	657	660
811 India Ivory/Tropical Turquoise	654	657	660
812 Surf Green/Highland Green	655	658	661
813 India Ivory/Surf Green	655	658	661
814 India Ivory/Coronado Yellow	654	657	660
815 Colonial Cream/Onyx Black	654	657	660
816 Colonial Cream/India Ivory	654	657	660
817 India Ivory/Canyon Coral	654	657	660
818 Adobe Beige/Sierra Gold	—	659	662
819 India Ivory/Matador Red	654	657	660

Interior Trim

Exterior Color	2102, 2103, 2113, 2154	2124		2109, 2119, 2129
820 Colonial Cream/Laurel Green		654	657	660
822 Dusk Pearl/Imperial Ivory		654	657	660

Bel Air Series

Interior Trim

Exterior Color	2402, 2403	2413, 2454	2409	2429	2434
793 Onyx Black	663	670	—	691	683
794 Imperial Ivory	669	—	690	697	683
795 Larkspur Blue	665	—	686	693	679
796 Harbor Blue	665	672	686	693	679
797 Surf Green	664	671	685	692	678
798 Highland Green	664	671	685	692	678
799 Tropical Turquoise	666	673	687	694	680
800 Colonial Cream	668	675	689	696	682
801 Canyon Coral	—	—	—	—	677
802 Matador Red	669	—	690	697	683
803 Coronado Yellow	—	—	—	—	677
804 Inca Silver	669	—	690	697	683
805 Sierra Gold	667	674	688	695	681
806 Adobe Beige	667	674	688	695	681
821 Dusk Pearl	—	—	—	—	677
823 Laurel Green	—	—	—	—	677
807 India Ivory/Onyx Black	676	669	690	697	—
808 Imperial Ivory/Inca Silver	676	669	690	697	—
809 Larkspur Blue/Harbor Blue	672	665	685	692	—

810 India Ivory/ Larkspur Blue	672	665	686	693	—
811 India Ivory/ Tropical Turquoise	673	666	687	694	—
812 Surf Green/ Highland Green	671	664	685	692	—
813 India Ivory/ Surf Green	671	664	685	692	—
814 India Ivory/ Coronado Yellow	670	663	684	691	—
815 Colonial Cream/Onyx Black	675	668	689	696	—
816 Colonial Cream/India Ivory	675	668	689	696	—
817 India Ivory/ Canyon Coral	670	663	684	691	—
818 Adobe Beige/Sierra Gold	674	667	688	695	—
819 India Ivory/ Matador Red	676	669	690	697	—
820 Colonial Cream/Laurel Green	670	663	684	691	—
822 Dusk Pearl/ Imperial Ivory	670	663	689	691	—

Convertible Top Colors
Black
Ivory
Green
Blue
Beige

Facts
Although the 1957 Chevrolet wasn't a totally new car, as the 1955 was, it received an extensive facelift, sharing only the same basic roof design, doors, and rear deck with the 1955–56 models. The front end featured a new integral bumper-grille combination and a lower,

flatter hood with two wind splits. The cowl air intakes were eliminated, and replacement air intakes were located in the upper half of the headlamp bezels. The front fenders also got three indentations just behind the headlight bezels. These were left empty on the 150s and 210s but were filled in with gold anodized aluminum on the Bel Airs. In the rear, the fenders incorporated fins and the taillight and back-up light location was incorporated in the bumper. The fuel filler door was located behind a panel on the left rear fender molding. Side trim on the 150s was similar to that found on the 1956 models, but on the 210s and Bel Airs, side styling was accentuated by a long molding that began on the front fender and gently sloped toward the rear bumper. Beneath the rear side windows, another molding continued straight to the rear, creating a triangular area. The triangular area was painted a second color if two-tone paint was used on the 210s, whereas on the Bel Airs, it was filled in with a brushed aluminum panel. Overall, the 1957 models were 2½in longer and 1½in lower.

As with the 1956 models, a large chromed *V* was located beneath Chevrolet script on the hood and rear deck if the car was equipped with one of the optional V-8 engines.

The interior was also restyled, with a single large round speedometer flanked by a smaller round temperature gauge on its left and a gasoline gauge on its right. Warning lights were still used for the generator and oil pressure functions. The glove compartment continued to be in the center of the dash, but speakers on cars equipped with a radio were relocated to the top of the dash.

The 150 Series was offered in two- and four-door sedans, a two-door utility sedan, a two-door Handyman station wagon, and a sedan delivery. Interiors were finished in a black and gray cloth/black vinyl combination, except in the wagon, where they came only in vinyl. As in 1956, the 150s came only with bright moldings around the windshield and rear window. Niceties such as foam seats, armrests, assist straps, a right side window visor were absent on the 150 Series, although an ashtray finally became standard equipment.

The 210s were available as two- and four-door sedans; a two-door Delray club coupe; a two-door sport coupe; a four-door sport sedan; a two-door Handyman station wagon; a four-door, six-passenger Townsman station wagon; and a four-door, nine-passenger Beauville station wagon. A cloth-and-vinyl combination was used in the interior, except in the Delray and wagons, which came in all-vinyl only. As before, the 210s came with more exterior bright trim and standard features.

The top-of-the-line Bel Airs came in two- and four-door sedans; a two-door sport coupe; a four-door sport sedan; a four-door, six-passenger Beauville station wagon; a two-door Nomad wagon; and a convertible. Besides the additional standard Bel Air features carried over from 1956, the 1957 Bel Airs were further set off by the use of a gold anodized front grille mesh, the previously mentioned gold simulated louvers on the front fenders, and rear deck accents. The Chevrolet and Bel Air script was also finished in gold. Bel Airs built before November 1 used gold-plated trim, whereas later cars got gold anodized aluminum.

Optional on the Bel Airs was a rear deck lid molding that matched the molding used on the Bel Air rear fenders.

The 1957 Nomad shared all the regular Bel Air features. Besides the distinctive Nomad styling, it did not come in any special exterior trim to set it off, with the exception of a small gold *V* on V-8–equipped examples.

The engine choice expanded in 1957. The Blue Flame six remained at 140hp, but it came with a different air cleaner and the water inlet was moved to the side in order to accommodate the lower hoodline.

Only one version of the 265ci small-block, rated at 162hp, was available. Replacing the other 265ci V-8s was an enlarged version of the small-block displacing 283ci. This was achieved by increasing the bore size to 3.875in. Both small-blocks benefited from fuel filters, larger cylinder head intake ports, wider main bearings, and a revised block casting. A new window-type distributor that was used for the first time made it possible to adjust the breaker points while the engine was running.

Besides the 265ci V-8, a two-barrel single-exhaust 283ci V-8 was rated at 185hp and was available only with automatic transmissions. A four-barrel version had a higher compression ratio—9.5:1 versus 8.5:1—for a 220hp output. Dual four-barrel 283s were available in either 245hp or 270hp trim, the difference attributed to a more radical mechanical-lifter camshaft on the 270hp version.

The big deal in 1957 was the availability of a Rochester mechanical fuel injection system on the 283ci V-8. It was offered in two horsepower ratings: 250hp for a hydraulic cam version and 283hp for the solid-lifter version. Compression ratio on the 283hp engine was 10.5:1.

A total of 1,530 passenger Chevrolets were equipped with fuel injection in 1957.

Besides the Powerglide, an additional automatic was made available: the two-speed Turboglide. It provided for very smooth, almost unnoticeable shifts, but it proved unreliable.

Another important improvement was the availability of the Positraction limited-slip rear axle, which resulted in better poor-weather traction. Rear axle ratios were revised: 3.36:1 for automatics, 3.55:1 for the three-speed manual, and 4.11:1 for the overdrive, which was unchanged. All engines except the six-cylinder and two-barrel 265s and 283s came with three-finger coil spring pressure plates instead of a diaphragm type.

Dual-exhaust-equipped cars came with a balance tube, which resulted in slightly more power and a quieter exhaust system.

1957 150 Two-Door Wagon

1957 Bel Air Sport Sedan

This Sport Coupe is one of eight models in the Two-Ten series for 1957. The exterior trim on this car shows that it was equipped with the fuel-injected V-8 engine

The 283ci V-8 was available with a Rochester mechanical fuel injection system in 1957. The hydraulic cam version produced 250hp, while the solid-lifter version produced 283hp.

The standard wheel size was reduced to 14x5in with 7.50x14 tires. Other chassis improvements included relocated rear springs (moved farther outward), improved front suspension ball joints, a beefed-up frame, and stronger brake shoe pull-back springs.

This well-equipped 1957 Two-Ten Sport Coupe shows off the long, sleek styling of the '57, especially when fitted with rear wheelwell skirts.

1957 Bel Air Nomad Station Wagon

1957 Bel Air Convertible

1957 One-Fifty Sedan

1957 Bel Air Hardtop Coupe

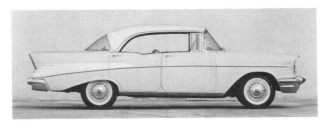

1957 Bel Air Hardtop Sedan

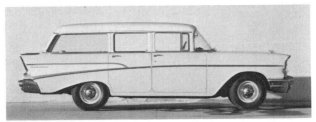

1957 Two-Ten Beauville 9-Passenger Station Wagon

Appendix

Production Dates

Listed below are the VINs of the cars produced each year at each plant. The numbers shown in each column are the last VINs produced at each plant for that particular month. Although they are estimates made by Classic Chevy Club International, they are correct for the great majority of cars built. However, the VINs shown for 1955 cars produced up to May 31, 1955, are exact. (Each year's VIN numbers are broken down into four chart sections of two or three months' production apiece.)

1955 Production

Plant	October 1954	November 1954	December 1954
Atlanta	9373	17746	26119
Baltimore	18359	35718	53077
Flint	20842	40684	60526
Janesville	18728	36456	54184
Kansas City	11276	21552	31828
Los Angeles	8703	16406	24109
Norwood	14597	28194	41791
Oakland	8865	16730	24595
St. Louis	21144	41288	61432
Tarrytown	22340	43680	65020

Plant	January 1955	February 1955	March 1955
Atlanta	34492	42865	51238
Baltimore	70436	87795	105154
Flint	80368	100210	120052
Janesville	71912	89640	107368
Kansas City	42104	52380	62656
Los Angeles	31812	39515	47218
Norwood	55388	68985	82582
Oakland	32640	40325	48190
St. Louis	81576	101720	121864
Tarrytown	86360	107700	129040

Plant	April 1955	May 1955	June 1955
Atlanta	59611	67984	78825
Baltimore	122513	139872	162369
Flint	139894	159736	185451
Janesville	125096	142824	165799
Kansas City	72932	83208	96525
Los Angeles	54921	62624	72607
Norwood	96179	109776	127398
Oakland	56055	63920	74113
St. Louis	142008	162152	188259
Tarrytown	150380	171720	199377

Plant	July 1955	August 1955
Atlanta	89686	100538
Baltimore	184867	207364
Flint	211166	236881
Janesville	188775	211750
Kansas City	109843	123161
Los Angeles	82590	92573
Norwood	145019	162641
Oakland	84306	94499
St. Louis	214365	240472
Tarrytown	227033	254690

1956 Production

Plant	October 1955	November 1955	December 1955
Atlanta	8682	16364	24046
Baltimore	16927	32854	48781
Flint	19206	37412	55618
Janesville	17266	33532	49798
Kansas City	10428	19856	29284
Los Angeles	8068	15136	22204
Norwood	13476	25952	38428
Oakland	8216	15432	22648
St. Louis	19482	37964	56446
Tarrytown	20580	40160	59740

Plant	January 1956	February 1956	March 1956
Atlanta	31728	39410	47092
Baltimore	64708	80635	96562
Flint	73824	92030	110236
Janesville	66064	82330	98596
Kansas City	38712	48140	57568
Los Angeles	29272	36340	43408
Norwood	50904	63380	75856
Oakland	29864	37080	44296
St. Louis	74928	93410	111892
Tarrytown	79320	98900	118480

Plant	April 1956	May 1956	June 1956
Atlanta	54774	62456	72442
Baltimore	112489	128416	149121
Flint	128442	146648	170316
Janesville	114862	131128	152274
Kansas City	66996	76424	88680
Los Angeles	50476	57544	66732
Norwood	88332	100808	117027
Oakland	51512	58728	68108
St. Louis	130374	148856	172883
Tarrytown	138060	157640	183094

Plant	July 1956	August 1956
Atlanta	82429	92415
Baltimore	169826	190531
Flint	193984	217652
Janesville	173420	194566
Kansas City	100937	113193
Los Angeles	75920	85109
Norwood	133246	149465
Oakland	77489	86870
St. Louis	196909	220936
Tarrytown	208548	234002

1957 Production

Plant	October 1956	November 1956	December 1956
Atlanta	107391	114782	122173

Baltimore	115324	130648	145972
Flint	117515	135030	152545
Janesville	115649	131298	146947
Kansas City	109071	118141	127213
Los Angeles	106799	113598	120397
Norwood	112002	124004	136006
Oakland	106942	113884	120826
St. Louis	117781	135562	153343
Tarrytown	118837	137674	156611

Plant	January 1957	February 1957	March 1957
Atlanta	129564	136995	144346
Baltimore	161296	176620	191944
Flint	170060	187575	205090
Janesville	162596	178245	193894
Kansas City	136284	145355	154426
Los Angeles	127196	133995	140794
Norwood	148008	160010	172012
Oakland	127768	134710	142652
St. Louis	171124	188905	206686
Tarrytown	175348	194185	213022

Plant	April 1957	May 1957	June 1957
Atlanta	151737	159128	168736
Baltimore	207268	222592	242513
Flint	222605	240120	262890
Janesville	209543	225192	245536
Kansas City	163497	172568	184360
Los Angeles	147593	154392	163231
Norwood	184014	196016	211619
Oakland	148594	155536	164561
St. Louis	224467	242248	265363
Tarrytown	231859	250696	275184

Plant	July 1957	August 1957
Atlanta	178345	187949
Baltimore	262434	282356
Flint	285659	308429
Janesville	265879	286223
Kansas City	196153	207945
Los Angeles	172069	180908

Plant	July 1957	August 1957
Norwood	227221	242824
Oakland	173585	182610
St. Louis	288479	311594
Tarrytown	299672	324160

1955–57 V-8 Exhaust Manifolds

Manifold Casting No.

Year	Engine	Left	Right	No. of Studs	Heat Riser No.
1955	265ci 162/180hp	3704791	3704792	2	3721509
1956	265ci 162/170/205hp	3704791	3704792	2	3725981
1956 early	265ci 225hp	3725563	3725563	2	3725981
1956 late	265ci 225hp	3731557	3731558	3	3731396
1957	265ci 162hp	3733975	3733976	3	3734204
	283ci 185/220hp	3733975	3733976	3	3734204
	283ci 245/270hp	3733975	3733976	3	3734204
	283ci 250/283hp	3733975	3733976*	3	3737631†

*Not drilled for heat choke tube.
†Spacer.

1955–57 Fisher Body and Chevrolet Model Numbers Interchange

Chevrolet	Fisher Body	Description	Model Year
150 Series			
1502	1211	2dr sedan	1955–57
1503	1219	4dr sedan	1955–57
1508	1271	2dr sedan delivery	1955–57
1512	1211B	2dr utility sedan	1955–57

| 1529 | 1263F | 2dr Handyman station wagon, 6 passenger | 1955–57 |

210 Series

2102	1011	2dr sedan	1955–57
2103	1019	4dr sedan	1955–57
2109	1062F	4dr Townsman station wagon, 6 passenger	1955–57
2113	1039	4dr hardtop sport sedan	1956–57
2119	1062FC	4dr Beauville station wagon, 9 passenger	1956–57
2124	1011A	2dr Delray club coupe	1955–57
2129	1063F	2dr Handyman station wagon, 6 passenger	1955–57
2154	1037	2dr hardtop sport coupe	1955–57

Bel Air Series

2402	1011D	2dr sedan	1955–57
2403	1019D	4dr sedan	1955–57
2409	1062DF	4dr Beauville station wagon, 6 passenger	1955, 1957
2413	1039D	4dr hardtop sport sedan	1956–57
2419	1062DF	4dr Beauville station wagon, 9 passenger	1956
2429	1064DF	2dr Nomad station wagon, 6 passenger	1955–57
2434	1067D	2dr convertible	1955–57
2454	1037D	2dr hardtop sport coupe	1955–57

1956–57 Dual Four-Barrel Carburetors

Optional during 1956–57 on the Chevrolet passenger cars was a dual four-barrel intake setup on the small-block V-8 engine. In 1956, the 265ci engine was rated at 225hp. In 1957, the dual four-barrel carburetors were offered only on the 283ci V-8 in two horsepower ratings: 245hp and 270hp, the 270hp version getting a high-performance mechanical-lifter camshaft. The dual four-barrel setup continued to be available only on the Corvette until 1961.

The carburetors used on all applications were Carter Model Wrought Cast Four Barrels (WCFBs). Both front and rear carburetors were similar except that the rear unit used a choke assembly. The black Bakelite cover on the housing stated Carter Climatic Control.

All carburetors were tagged with a triangular identification tag like this:

The code on the identification tag broke down as follows:

A—Carburetor number

B—Blank or inspector's punch

C—Date code, with each month represented by a letter, *A* through *M*, and one or two digits for the date; for example, A9 would decode to January 9

D, E—Inspector's punch

This identification tag may be missing. If so, you can identify the carburetor through the various numbers cast on the throttle body and air horn. However, the 1956 and early 1957 units were different from those used on late 1957 engines.

The 1956 and early 1957 carburetors were Carter 2419S units in the front and 2362S units in the rear. These were equipped with an idle air adjustment screw, which was located on the left rear of the throttle body. This screw was used to set idle speed, as the throttle valves were closed at idling speed. Air-fuel mixture screws were located on the front of the throttle body.

During 1957, 2419S and 2362S carburetors were replaced with 2626S units in the front and 2627S units in the rear. These carburetors did not have the rear idle air adjustment screw. Early and late versions differed as well. Early 2627S carburetors came with a thin 0.29in auxiliary air valve weight, whereas the 2626S carburetor came with a thicker and heavier 0.5in weight. Late 2626S and 2627S carburetors used a shorter 1.4in-combined-length auxiliary air valve lever weight.

The 2626S and 2627S units have been found on both 245hp and 270hp engines. In addition, Carter lists carburetors 2613S and 2614S for use on the 270hp engine, and these were installed on the 1958–61 Corvette 270hp engines.

1956–57 Carter 2419S, 2362S
Throttle body casting—1-1387A
Air horn cover, early 1956—6-1114 or 6-1122
Air horn cover, late 1956 & early 1957—6-1151 or 6-1203
Most, but not all, air horn castings were also stamped on the left of the casting number with the following:

Horn Casting Number	Stamping Number
6-1114	1114
6-1122	1122
6-1151	1161 front; 1156 rear
6-1203	1161 front; 1156 rear

Late 1957 Carter 2626S, 2627S, 2613S, 2614S
Throttle body casting—1-1387B
Air horn cover—6-1299
Air horn stamping—1161 front; 1296 rear

Engine Identification
All Chevrolet engines have a number stamped on them to identify them. This number is known as the engine serial number. The 1955–56 cars used a ten- or eleven-digit number to identify the engine, whereas from 1957 on, Chevrolet switched to a six- or seven-digit number.

1955–56
In 1955–56, the engine serial number consisted of a unit number, the engine plant code, a two-digit number indicating the model year, and the engine's suffix code. Engine plant codes were as follows:
F—Flint
T—Tonawanda
The engine serial number on V-8 engines was stamped on a pad on the right (passenger's) side of the

engine block just where the cylinder head and block met. On the six-cylinder engine, it was stamped on the right-hand side of the cylinder block at the rear of the distributor.

As an example, 001001F55GC would decode as follows:

001001—Unit number

F—Plant designation (Flint)

55—Model year (1955)

GC—Engine suffix (265ci V-8 with overdrive transmission)

1957

For 1957 and later engines, the identification number was changed. As an example, F0126 G would break down as follows:

F—Plant designation (Flint)

0126—Production date and month

G—Engine suffix (265ci V-8 with 3-speed transmission)

The unit number was dropped, the plant designation stayed the same, and a production date and month replaced the model year. Months were designated by a two-digit number from 01 through 12 (01 for January, 02 for February, etc.), and a two-digit number indicated the day of the month (01 for the first day of the month, 02 for the second day of the month, etc.). The engine suffix remained unchanged. This number was stamped in the same places as before on both the six- and eight-cylinder engines.

Transmission Identification

After the engine, the transmission is the next major component that should be checked. The 1955–56 transmissions carried an identification number that consisted of a plant prefix letter that stood for the transmission plant, and a production date.

The following are plant prefix letters:

Prefix	Plant	Transmission Type
B	Toledo	Turboglide (1957 only)
C	Cleveland	Powerglide
M	Muncie	3-speed & overdrive
S	Saginaw	3-speed & overdrive

For example, M605 would decode to a Muncie three-speed built on June 5. C213 would decode to a Cleveland Powerglide built on February 13.

For 1957, on the Powerglide and Turboglide automatic transmissions only, the transmission identification number was changed to include the shift in which the unit was built. The letter *D* indicated day shift and the letter *N* indicated night shift. These letters were added to the identification number right after the production date. For example, C213D would decode to a Cleveland Powerglide built on February 13 during the day shift.

The location of the transmission identification number was as follows:

3-speed manual—Stamped on the rear face of the case on the upper right corner

Powerglide—Stamped on the rear face of the case on the lower right corner

Turboglide—Stamped on the rear face of the case on the lower right corner

Rear Axle Identification

Rear axle identification numbers were stamped on the front, right side of the differential carrier. They consisted of a plant designation and a four-digit number consisting of the month and date. Plant designations broke down as follows:

| | Plant | |
| | Gear & | |
Description	Axle	Buffalo
3-speed manual, 3.7:1 ratio (1955–56)	AA	BA
3-speed manual, 3.55:1 ratio (1957)	AA	BA
3-speed, 3.55:1 close-ratio, (1957)	AA	BA
Automatic, 3.55:1 ratio (1955–56)	AB	BB
Automatic, 3.36:1 ratio (1957)	AB	BB
Overdrive, 4.11:1 ratio (1955–57)	AC	BC
Limited slip, 3.55:1 ratio (1957)	AK	—
Limited slip, 4.11:1 ratio (1957)	AL	—
Limited slip, 3.36:1 ratio (1957)	AM	—

For example, AA212 would decode to a three-speed manual built on February 12 at Gear and Axle.

Engine Casting Date Codes

Although it is beyond the scope of this book to list all engine part casting numbers, it is useful to be able to decode the date a part was cast. Most parts used on an engine should predate the assembly date code of the engine and should be within thirty days of engine assembly. Exceptions exist, of course, such as for parts cast for use at a later date or in a later model year.

Engine casting date codes consisted of three or four digits. They began with a letter for the month (*A* for January through *L* for December). Next came a number standing for the date of the month, and last was a number standing for the last digit of the model year. For example, B227 would stand for February 22, 1957.

The date code was located on the right- (passenger's-) side rear on six-cylinder and small-block V-8 engines.

In much the same way, subsidiary parts, such as manifolds, carried a similar casting date.

Cowl Tags

An important way to identify a 1955–57 Chevrolet is by the cowl tag. This was a thin aluminum sheet metal tag with stamped numbers and letters that was located on the right side of the cowl in the engine compartment.

The cowl tag contained four basic pieces of information: style number (model year, series, and type), body number, trim number, and paint number. Underneath the last designation, the paint number, was a space for convertible tops (Top) and accessories (ACC).

A typical cowl tag was like this:

Style No.	55-1037D
Body No.	S32923
Trim No.	522
Paint No.	612

This plate would decode as follows:

Style—This was a 1955 Chevrolet Bel Air sport coupe. The model number is the Fisher body number rather than the Chevrolet model number, which in this case is 2454.

Body No.—This was the 32,923rd Chevrolet built at the St. Louis plant.

Trim No.—This Bel Air had a beige cloth/turquoise vinyl interior.

Paint No.—This Bel Air was painted in India Ivory/Regal Turquoise two-tone.

Basic Specifications

1955

Measurements	1502, 1512, 2102, 2124, 2402, 1503, 2103, 2403	1529, 2129, 2109, 2409
Length (in)	195.6	197.1
Wheelbase (in)	115.0	115.0
Height (in)*	62.1	62.1
Width (in)	73.4	73.4
Front tread (in)	58.0	58.0
Rear tread (in)	58.8	58.8
Road clearance (in)†	8.0	8.0

*Unloaded.
†Under rear axle center.

Measurements	2434, 2154, 2454	1508, 2429
Length (in)	195.6	197.1
Wheelbase (in)	115.0	115.0
Height (in)*	60.4	62.1/60.7
Width (in)	73.4	73.4
Front tread (in)	58.0	58.0
Rear tread (in)	58.8	58.8
Road clearance (in)†	8.0	8.0

*Unloaded.
†Under rear axle center.

Fuel Capacity
Station wagon sedan delivery—17gal
All others—16gal

1956

Measurements	1502, 1503, 1512, 2102, 2103, 2124, 2402, 2403	1529, 2109, 2119, 2129, 2419
Length (in)	115.0	115.0
Wheelbase (in)	197.5	200.8
Height (in)*	62.0	62.0

	72.5	72.5
Width (in)	72.5	72.5
Front tread (in)	58.0	58.0
Rear tread (in)	58.9	58.9
Road clearance (in)†	8.0	8.0

*Unloaded.
†Under rear axle center.

Measurements	2154, 2434, 2454	1508
Length (in)	115.0	115.0
Wheelbase (in)	197.5	200.8
Height (in)*	60.7	62.0
Width (in)	72.5	72.5
Front tread (in)	58.0	58.0
Rear tread (in)	58.9	58.9
Road clearance (in)†	8.0	8.0

*Unloaded.
†Under rear axle center.

Measurements	2113, 2413	2429
Length (in)	115.0	115.0
Wheelbase (in)	197.5	200.8
Height (in)*	60.6	60.8
Width (in)	72.5	72.5
Front tread (in)	58.0	58.0
Rear tread (in)	58.9	58.9
Road clearance (in)†	8.0	8.0

*Unloaded.
†Under rear axle center.

Fuel Capacity
Station wagon sedan delivery—17gal
All others—16gal

1957

Measurement	1502, 1503, 1512, 2102, 2103, 2124, 2403	1529, 2109, 2119, 2129, 2409
Length (in)	115.0	115.0
Wheelbase (in)	200.0	200.0
Height (in)*	61.49	61.45
Width (in)	73.86	73.86
Front tread (in)	58.0	58.0
Rear tread (in)	58.8	58.8
Road clearance (in)†	7.57	7.57

*Unloaded.
†Under rear axle center.

Measurements	2434	2154, 2454
Length (in)	115.0	115.0
Wheelbase (in)	200.0	200.0
Height (in)*	59.63	60.09
Width (in)	73.86	73.86
Front tread (in)	58.0	58.0
Rear tread (in)	58.8	58.8
Road clearance (in)†	7.57	7.57

*Unloaded.
†Under rear axle center.

Measurements	2113, 2413	2429	1508
Length (in)	115.0	115.0	115.0
Wheelbase (in)	200.0	200.0	200.0
Height (in)*	59.98	60.22	61.63
Width (in)	73.86	73.86	73.86
Front tread (in)	58.0	58.0	58.0
Rear tread (in)	58.8	58.8	58.8
Road clearance (in)†	7.57	7.57	7.57

*Unloaded.
†Under rear axle center.

Fuel Capacity
Station wagon sedan delivery—17gal
All others—16gal

Vehicle Curb Weights

1955

The following weights consist of the vehicle weight plus the weight of gasoline (97lb) and the weight of water (33lb). In all cases, the standard six-cylinder engine and manual transmission were used. For V-8 engines, deduct 30lb from the total, and for automatic transmissions, add 95lb.

Model	Description	Weight (Lb)
150 Series		
1502	2dr sedan	3,240
1503	4dr sedan	3,295
1508	2dr sedan delivery	3,240
1512	2dr utility sedan	3,215
1529	2dr Handyman station wagon	3,420

210 Series

2102	2dr sedan	3,275
2103	4dr sedan	3,310
2109	4dr Townsman station wagon	3,500
2124	2dr Delray club coupe	3,275
2129	2dr Handyman station wagon	3,460
2154	2dr hardtop sport coupe	3,315

Bel Air Series

2402	2dr sedan	3,285
2403	4dr sedan	3,330
2409	4dr Beauville station wagon	3,515
2429	2dr Nomad station wagon	3,495
2434	2dr convertible	3,445
2454	2dr hardtop sport coupe	3,325

1956

The following weights consist of the vehicle weight plus the weight of gasoline (102lb) and the weight of water (33lb), except for the sedan deliverys and station wagons, where they include 105lb for gasoline and 33lb for water. In all cases, the standard six-cylinder engine and manual transmission were used. For V-8 engines, deduct 20lb from the total, and for automatic transmissions, add 95lb.

Model	Description	Weight (Lb)

150 Series

1502	2dr sedan	3,300
1503	4dr sedan	3,340
1508	2dr sedan delivery	3,285
1512	2dr utility sedan	3,260
1529	2dr Handyman station wagon	3,450

210 Series

2102	2dr sedan	3,310
2103	4dr sedan	3,345
2109	4dr Townsman station wagon	3,530
2113	4dr hardtop sport sedan	3,395
2119	4dr Beauville station wagon	3,635
2124	2dr Delray club coupe	3,315
2129	2dr Handyman station wagon	3,485
2154	2dr hardtop sport coupe	3,340

Bel Air Series

2402	2dr sedan	3,330
2403	4dr sedan	3,365
2413	4dr hardtop sport sedan	3,415
2419	4dr Beauville station wagon	3,650
2429	2dr Nomad station wagon	3,500
2434	2dr convertible	3,475
2454	2dr hardtop sport coupe	3,365

1957

The following weights consist of the vehicle weight plus the weight of gasoline (102lb) and the weight of water (33lb), except for the sedan deliverys and station wagons, where they include 105lb for gasoline and 33lb for water.

Model	Description	Weight (Lb)
150 Series		
1502	2dr sedan A	3,350
	2dr sedan A, P	3,429
	2dr sedan B	3,332
	2dr sedan C, P	3,424
	2dr sedan C, T	3,350
1503	4dr sedan A	3,375
	4dr sedan A, P	3,472
	4dr sedan B	3,375
	4dr sedan C, P	3,476
	4dr sedan C, T	3,375
1508	2dr sedan delivery A	3,357
	2dr sedan delivery A, P	3,445
	2dr sedan delivery B	3,358
	2dr sedan delivery C, P	3,476
	2dr sedan delivery C, T	3,357
1512	2dr utility sedan A	3,302
	2dr utility sedan A, P	3,398
	2dr utility sedan B	3,325
	2dr utility sedan C, P	3,417
	2dr utility sedan C, T	3,302
1529	2dr Handyman station wagon A	3,549
	2dr Handyman station wagon A, P	3,621
	2dr Handyman station wagon B	3,510
	2dr Handyman station wagon C, P	3,606
	2dr Handyman station wagon C, T	3,549

210 Series

2102	2dr sedan A	3,364
	2dr sedan A, P	3,449
	2dr sedan B	3,361
	2dr sedan C, P	3,447
	2dr sedan C, T	3,364
2103	4dr sedan A	3,409
	4dr sedan A, P	3,505
	4dr sedan B	3,407
	4dr sedan C, P	3,483
	4dr sedan C, T	3,409
2109	4dr Townsman station wagon A	3,607
	4dr Townsman station wagon A, P	3,691
	4dr Townsman station wagon B	3,603
	4dr Townsman station wagon C, P	3,687
	4dr Townsman station wagon C, T	3,607
2113	4dr hardtop sport sedan A	3,459
	4dr hardtop sport sedan A, P	3,560
	4dr hardtop sport sedan B	3,449
	4dr hardtop sport sedan C, P	3,554
	4dr hardtop sport sedan C, T	3,459
2119	4dr Beauville station wagon A	3,704
	4dr Beauville station wagon A, P	3,808
	4dr Beauville station wagon B	3,708
	4dr Beauville station wagon C, P	3,815
	4dr Beauville station wagon C, T	3,704
2124	2dr Delray club coupe A	3,359
	2dr Delray club coupe A, P	3,438
	2dr Delray club coupe B	3,354
	2dr Delray club coupe C, P	3,444
	2dr Delray club coupe C, T	3,359
2129	2dr Handyman station wagon A	3,549
	2dr Handyman station wagon A, P	3,643
	2dr Handyman station wagon B	3,550
	2dr Handyman station wagon C, P	3,642
	2dr Handyman station wagon C, T	3,549
2154	2dr hardtop sport coupe A	3,399
	2dr hardtop sport coupe A, P	3,499
	2dr hardtop sport coupe B	3,394
	2dr hardtop sport coupe C, P	3,489
	2dr hardtop sport coupe C, T	3,399

Bel Air Series

2402	2dr sedan A	3,371
	2dr sedan A, P	3,468
	2dr sedan B	3,365
	2dr sedan C, P	3,467
	2dr sedan C, T	3,371
2403	4dr sedan A	3,415
	4dr sedan A, P	3,514
	4dr sedan B	3,413
	4dr sedan C, P	3,504
	4dr sedan C, T	3,415
2409	4dr Beauville station wagon A	3,603
	4dr Beauville station wagon A, P	3,703
	4dr Beauville station wagon B	3,608
	4dr Beauville station wagon C, P	3,704
	4dr Beauville station wagon C, T	3,603
2413	4dr hardtop sport sedan A	3,481
	4dr hardtop sport sedan A, P	3,579
	4dr hardtop sport sedan B	3,467
	4dr hardtop sport sedan C, P	3,592
	4dr hardtop sport sedan C, T	3,481
2429	2dr Nomad station wagon A	3,599
	2dr Nomad station wagon A, P	3,698
	2dr Nomad station wagon B	3,598
	2dr Nomad station wagon C, P	3,683
	2dr Nomad station wagon C, T	3,599
2434	2dr convertible A	3,560
	2dr convertible A, P	3,650
	2dr convertible B	3,541
	2dr convertible C, P	3,653
	2dr convertible C, T	3,560
2454	2dr hardtop sport coupe A	3,427
	2dr hardtop sport coupe A, P	3,509
	2dr hardtop sport coupe B	3,396
	2dr hardtop sport coupe C, P	3,514
	2dr hardtop sport coupe C, T	3,427

Note:
P—Powerglide
T—Turboglide
A—235ci 6cyl
B—265ci V-8
C—283ci V-8